'Deft, witty and profound, this is a true story about how to let go, and when to hold on. Jean Hannah Edelstein's writing glows with a peerless clarity that had me turning the pages all night. A stunning book'   Jessie Burton

'Jean Hannah Edelstein is one of the most brilliant writers of her generation, as witty, wry and unsentimental as Nora Ephron. This is a magnificent book, about families, mortality, love and the hard, necessary work of becoming an adult'   Olivia Laing

'Edelstein's memoir takes us into the biographies of her father and grandfather, and the decade prior to her father's death – her professional struggles, romantic encounters and attempts to settle somewhere she can call home. It is an unsentimental, unflinching account of dealing with grief told with honesty, self-effacing wit and poignancy'   Hannah Beckerman, *Observer*

'As enthralling as fiction, this memoir hits you with hard truths from the outset. Edelstein describes rebuilding her life after her father dies, and at the same time facing the uncomfortable, annoying realities of adulthood'   *Elle*

'Never sentimental, this memoir is by turns extremely funny and extremely sad; Edelstein is a wonderful writer, and this is a stunning book'   *Stylist*

'Edelstein's memoir is a work of deceptive simplicity and heart-crushing truths . . . by the end, you'll never want to let her go'
                                                            Sarra Manning, *Red*

'A most magnificent, beautifully written memoir. Unsentimental but heartbreaking, the voice – true and clear. Brilliant'
                                         Nina Stibbe, author of *Love, Nina*

'The American-born author details her literal and figurative journey with wit, charm and zest. But there is heartbreak too . . . Yet Edelstein continues to bounce back, and it's with deep regret that you turn the last page of her hugely entertaining and affecting account'   *The Lady*

'A very funny and charming and bittersweet book'

Jami Attenberg, author of *All Grown Up*

'Jean Hannah Edelstein is an exceptional writer, simultaneously wry and heartbreaking. She has this incredible ability to extrapolate moments of grace and sadness from the everyday. And this memoir about cancer, mortality, shifting ideas of home and love is no exception'

Nikesh Shukla

'This isn't the heroic narrative about a fight for life against the odds, but instead it's about getting on with things, maybe not in the most heroic way, but in a way that's funny and real and quietly profound. *This Really Isn't About You* is wry and poignant and true, and I loved it'

Julie Cohen, author of *Together*

'A bold and unusual meditation on loss, instability, freedom and home. Engrossing, funny and brave'

Kate Murray-Browne, author of *The Upstairs Room*

'Insightful and charming, this is a breathtaking exploration of grief and becoming'   Laura Jane Williams, author of *Becoming*

'*This Really Isn't About You* really isn't about me, but it resonated in all sorts of ways: as a woman, as a writer, as a daughter. It is funny and serious, moving yet entirely unsentimental, and bracingly truthful. Jean Hannah Edelstein considers life in all its complexity with great clarity, grace and wit'

Lisa Owens, author of *Not Working*

'Jean Hannah Edelstein has written an elegant, beautiful book about a time in her life that was messy and ugly. It's strange to say such a sad story was "a joy", but her gift as a writer is that it was'

Emma Forrest, author of *Your Voice in My Head*

This Really Isn't About You

Jean Hannah Edelstein is a writer who lives in Brooklyn. She writes regularly for the *Guardian* and other outlets, and a weekly newsletter, which *Vogue* said 'pops up in your inbox like lucid dreaming.' She also writes marketing emails for tech companies, so you've probably deleted her work. *This Really Isn't About You* is her first memoir.

Jean Hannah Edelstein

This Really Isn't About You

WITHDRAWN

PICADOR

First published 2018 by Picador

First published in paperback 2018 by Picador

This edition published 2019 by Picador
an imprint of Pan Macmillan
20 New Wharf Road, London N1 9RR
Associated companies throughout the world
www.panmacmillan.com

ISBN 978-1-5098-6381-5

1 3 5 7 9 8 6 4 2

A CIP catalogue record for this book is available from the British Library.

Typeset in 11.52/15.55 pt Dante MT Std by Jouve (UK), Milton Keynes
Printed and bound by CPI Group (UK) Ltd, Croydon, CR0 4YY

Visit **www.picador.com** to read more about all our books
and to buy them. You will also find features, author interviews and
news of any author events, and you can sign up for e-newsletters
so that you're always first to hear about our new releases.

For my mother, with love and gratitude

'Because if I tell the story, it doesn't hurt as much. Because if I tell the story, I can get on with it.'

Nora Ephron – *Heartburn*

BETWEEN

1

I was in Brooklyn looking for love on OKCupid when my father died. It was a cold February night in 2014. It was almost two years after the night in late spring when my parents called me on Skype – I was at home in London, and they were at home in Baltimore – and Dad looked into the camera and said: I have lung cancer.

That night in February, I had a rare feeling of contentment, or something like it. After six weeks of not quite having a home, of living between my parents' house in Baltimore and a temporary spot in Brooklyn, I'd secured a lease on an apartment in a brownstone in Clinton Hill, a pretty neighbourhood in the middle of Brooklyn. I was beginning to feel like it might be time to build my real life in America. Maybe, I thought, I could start working on finding a boyfriend. The other two things were in place: I had a job, and now I had a place to live. Maybe my life was almost under control.

Getting the lease to my new apartment had not been easy. Until six weeks earlier, when I'd moved to New York City, I had spent all of my adult life outside of the United States, where I'd grown up: in Montreal, Dublin, London, Berlin. This made getting a lease not a chore, but an ordeal. All of the credit-card debt I amassed when I lived abroad counted for nothing to American creditors. It wasn't that my credit rating was bad. It was zero. To the systems that control money in America, I did not exist. No one would give me a lease on my own. I was a thirty-two-year-old woman, an independent woman, and yet I needed to ask my dad for help. He had agreed to be the guarantor on my new apartment, to sign documents to promise that if I failed to pay the rent he would be held accountable for my delinquency. But the final agreement had been delayed, because my father didn't like the requests that the letting agency was making. They were asking him to disclose all kinds of personal financial information. My father thought that this went too far.

Over the course of the previous weekend, Dad and I had discussed the circumstances several times on the phone, and over Skype. I was feeling a little impatient that he was being inflexible. It felt old-fashioned. I had moved to New York City, back to the United States, to be close to him; to be near him and my mother. I appreciated that my father was helping me, knew that I was very lucky that he could help me. But I also felt frustrated.

The last time we spoke about the lease we were both on camera. I was at the kitchen table in the ground-floor studio apartment I was subletting from a friend. Dad was sitting in front of his laptop in his home office. His face was gaunt, but he was smiling. He was very sick, I knew he was, and so did he, but my parents hadn't yet started discussing the end, at least not with me. We had not talked about hospice care, or about making plans. I wasn't going to bring it up.

In that final call, Dad was wearing black braces because abdominal swelling from the spread of the cancer meant that his belt no longer fit.

I like your suspenders, I said.

Thanks, Dad said. I got them for a great deal on Amazon.

We discussed the lease. The sticking point was my father's tax returns. He did not want to send copies of them to the letting agency. It was an invasion of his privacy.

In fact, my father said, disclosing his income might put me in danger. That made me laugh, because although as far as I knew he and my mother were financially comfortable, I did not believe that my father had enough money to make his thirty-two-year-old daughter an appealing victim of a ransomed kidnapping in 2014.

The last time my father and I spoke about the lease was the last time that we spoke about anything. Had I known this was the case, and had someone said to me: Do you want to say something else, because this is your final conversation with your father? I'm not sure that I would have said anything different. I wouldn't have known what I was supposed to say.

Likewise, if someone had said to me: What would you like to be doing when your father dies? I would not have said, I would like to be looking for love on OKCupid. But I did not have the luxury to make that decision. Who does?

I'd like to tell you in my last conversation with my father I said I loved him, though the truth is I do not remember. The truth is that this was not a thing we said to each other very often, over the phone – my father and

I, or anyone in our immediate family. It was just not our usual practice, though my father did sign all of his emails and texts that way: *I'm waiting in the car outside the train station. Love, Dad.*

I didn't know that we would not speak again, but I did take a screenshot of our faces, in that final call. His the size of the screen. Mine small, in the lower right-hand corner. In the screenshot, our faces looked alike. Our love for each other was something, I have to believe, that my father and I both knew and trusted.

The apartment in Clinton Hill was not the best apartment that I'd seen. The living room didn't have any windows. The walls were painted a shade that could well have been called 'Charlotte Perkins Gilman Yellow'. The building was only about a hundred feet from the Brooklyn–Queens Expressway. It was far from the subway that I needed to take to work. In time, after I moved in, I would also learn that the apartment was full of mice, and that the tarmac handball court across the way doubled as an open-air drug market after dark. But it was the apartment that the real-estate agent had shown me with the fewest stairs to the front door. I chose it because I'd imagined that my father would be able to come with my mother to visit me in my new home in Brooklyn before he died. I'd imagined that he'd be able to climb those few stairs.

In the morning of the day he died my father and I had finally come to a resolution. We'd had an email exchange in which I agreed to tell the agent that it was not necessary for my dad to release his full tax returns, that no one should really make you release your full tax return under any circumstances. I had agreed that he was correct. In the last email he sent me, my dad wrote back: *Great! Love, Dad.* I smiled.

That morning, before or after we exchanged these emails, my father had also written another email to his doctor saying his abdominal pain was getting worse, that he was really not feeling well at all. The doctor said she was very sorry to hear that and suggested some new pain-relief options, but she did not suggest that he go to the hospital. Maybe this was for the best. My father's body had been broken by the cancer, by its spread, and if the doctor had suggested that my father should go to the hospital when he reported his pain, then perhaps he would not have died at home with my mother by his side, which is what happened that night while I was looking for love on OKCupid. My father tried to eat dinner, and then he told my mother that he was really not feeling well, and then he stood up from the easy chair where he had been spending most of his days for the last few weeks, and then he collapsed and died on the wooden floor in the space between the dining area and the family room.

His heart.

It ruptured.

I was told there was a lot of blood.

At that moment, when my father died, I was tucked under a duvet on a mattress on the floor. I had sublet the basement apartment unfurnished and had not yet acquired a bedframe. It seemed like a bad idea to own much until I had a more permanent place for my stuff. That winter, the winter of 2014, there was a weather pattern that had been diagnosed as a 'polar vortex', and a draught blew from where the air conditioner was installed in the wall to where my mattress was, a draught that could only be stopped by an air-conditioner cover that no longer existed. I was wearing American Apparel winter leggings and a thermal shirt and a thick handmade cream-coloured winter hat with a pompom. I'd bought the hat for fifty euros from a shop with clean white edges a few doors down from the apartment building where I lived in Berlin. I felt cosy, and content. It was the first time I had felt either of those feelings for some time.

On the OKCupid profile I built that night, I put up a photo I'd taken of myself standing by the window in the apartment in Berlin that I had moved out of a few weeks earlier. I'd filtered the photo in black and white to make me look younger and more pretty. I put up another photo of me standing in front of a graffiti-covered swan boat in an abandoned Berlin amusement park, where I had gone with some friends to celebrate my thirty-second birthday. I put up a third photograph of me holding my friend's dog in my lap while he was wearing a medical cone around his neck, so that it looked like I was holding a dog's head in a martini glass. I hoped that the photos represented the kind of person that I was, or who I wished to be: youngish, prettyish. An appreciator of things that are a little bit absurd. A lover of dogs. In the space for self-description, I wrote something about how I was new to New York. An ex-expat. A person who had not lived in the United States since the late 90s. A time-traveller from the Clinton years. I did not note the reason that I had returned to New York.

I did not write: I came back because my father is dying of lung cancer. But to the question about whether I could date a smoker, I replied: Absolutely not.

I posted my profile. I began correspondences with some men who offered themselves as candidates for whatever it was that I was looking for. What I was looking for was someone who would fall in love with me fast enough so that when my father died, my new boyfriend would be there to hold me while I cried myself to sleep. I didn't know about the email my father had sent to his doctor that morning. I knew that my father's health was dire, but I did not know how dire. Of love and death I wondered: which would move faster?

One man who sent me a message looked sort of handsome and though he was my age he was restarting his career, in his first year of medical school, which I admired. In high school, I had wanted to be a doctor, a dream that I'd abandoned once I got to university and got a C+ in my first science course. Now that my father was dying of lung cancer, I wanted to be a doctor even more.

Why did you move to New York? the medical student asked, and I wrote back, Well, I needed to be nearer my parents in Baltimore, and because he was a medical student, and therefore I assumed he could handle the truth, I continued.

My father has lung cancer, I wrote.

The medical student wrote back: I'm sorry to hear that.

I replied: Thank you, but under the circumstances he's doing well, and the medical student wrote: I'm glad to hear that.

And during the time we had that pleasant exchange of messages, my father had, in fact, died.

What area code do you want? my friend Elyse had emailed as I was preparing to return to New York – Elyse and I worked together, and she was in charge of organizing my company phone. I wrote back: 410, the Baltimore area code, so that it's a local call to my parents. Elyse replied kindly: Jean, that hasn't been a thing for years!

The last time there was such a thing as a long-distance call between cell phones in different area codes in America was ten years earlier, which was a time when I was not living in America, so how would I have known?

Make it 410 anyway, I wrote, and Elyse wrote, Sure.

And so that night when my phone rang with an unfamiliar 410 number – after I'd finished exchanging messages with the medical student, when I had closed my laptop and arranged my duvet and pillows to go to sleep – I looked at the unfamiliar number with the 410 area code and I thought, I'm sure if that's not a wrong number they'll leave a voicemail and I can call them back.

I went to sleep.

They didn't leave a voicemail but in the morning there was an email from my mother, sent at a small-hours time that my mother had never emailed me from before.

Call Arthur before you go to work, is what the email said.

(My mother had been awake all night. Around six o'clock that morning she had tried to lie down, tried to sleep, which is why she had told me to call my older brother.)

To get enough phone reception in the ground-floor apartment, I had to go to the window and open it and press myself against the burglar-proof bars as snow drifted through them. In California, where my brother was, it was a touch before four o'clock in the morning. When my brother answered his phone, I could hear that he was crying.

Jean, he said, it's very bad. It's very bad.

For a second I felt a desperate kind of hope that the bad thing was not the worst thing, just another very bad thing. But, of course, it wasn't.

I screamed, three times, a sound I'd never heard.

I called my friend Kylah, a friend I'd known since I was nine, who knew my father too. She was one of the few people in New York who I knew well. She came to the apartment and washed my dishes and bought me a train ticket to Baltimore while I cried and took a shower. In the shower, while crying, I thought: Maybe I should kill myself, and then I thought: Actually, I guess that is not the point of this at all.

On the Amtrak train to Baltimore, a trip that takes about three hours from New York City, I pressed my face against a dirty window and cried while listening to my father's favourite Mozart French horn concerto, one he'd played on Sunday mornings when making pancakes for the family. When the horn concerto finished, I started it again.

After my father had collapsed on the floor, after the blood, after my mother had called 911, some neighbours saw the ambulance and ran from their homes to help. The unknown phone number was the neighbour's cell phone. My mother had been trying to call me from the hospital, where the neighbours sat with her after my father's death was professionally confirmed. I can imagine why she didn't leave a voicemail.

My mother rode in the ambulance with my father to the hospital but he was already dead. When the neighbours took her home they asked if they could come inside and help her put the house back in order. My mother told me that she said: No. Thank you, no.

Later, my mother told me that cleaning up felt like the last thing she needed to do for him, and that she felt she needed to do it on her own. Maybe she also felt that she needed to do it for us: his children.

When I got to the house in Baltimore it was early in the afternoon. The wooden floor in the space between the dining room and family room was spotless.

2

His name was William Alan Edelstein. When he was a child people called him Billy, and later, people called him Bill. One time, long before he met my mother, when he was in graduate school, my father had a girlfriend who said she would prefer to call him by his Hebrew name, which was Gabriel. My father told me that story as an example of something that he found ridiculous.

My father was born in a small town in upstate New York, called Gloversville. The town was called Gloversville because the main industry was glove manufacturing. In fact, Gloversville was the heart of the American glove industry around the time that my father was born, in 1944. Which is why his family, and many other families of Jewish people, immigrants from Eastern Europe and their first-generation American children, moved to Gloversville from New York City: to make gloves, to make families.

When women and men stopped wearing gloves to be polite, in the 60s and 70s, the economy in Gloversville tanked, in the way that economies in so many American towns that were driven by manufacturing tanked. Still, my father always loved Gloversville. When I was small, he drove us to see the house where he lived with his grand-parents and his mother after his birth, because his father was away in Burma, fixing radios for the Army Air Force. By the time we got there the town was rough around the edges, emptying. But when we all sat together in the family car outside the gabled house where my father had started his life, he beamed.

When my father was three or four, my grandparents moved to Schenectady, New York, about sixty miles from Gloversville, where they lived in an apartment above a small grocery store and my father's sister, my aunt Barbara, was born. When my father was about seven his mother, my grandmother Hannah, was diagnosed with colon cancer. She was thirty-two years old. When my father was around twelve the family moved to Chicago so that my grandfather could work with his three brothers in their family business and so my grandmother could get better healthcare. When my father was seventeen his mother died. She was forty-two.

When my grandmother died, my father told me, no one warned him and his sister that she was dying. Adults told them that she was going to the hospital, and then they told them that she had died. I don't think my father had very clear memories of the time when his mother died, or if he did, he didn't want to talk about them. Many years later, in 2010, my father was diagnosed with Lynch syndrome, a genetic condition that gives people a high risk of colon cancer, among many other kinds of cancer. He realized that his mother had also had Lynch syndrome, though at the time of her death the condition didn't have a name. It was just a tragedy.

My father was a senior in high school when his mother

died, and that autumn he went to the University of Illinois to study physics, and then to Harvard, for graduate school.

When my father finished his Ph.D. at Harvard, he was thirty years old. He liked to make the point that he hadn't been a star student in graduate school – he liked to say that it took him nine years because he'd been 'messing around'. My father's Ph.D. was in nuclear physics, and when asked about his time at Harvard he would tell people how he would ride his bike through Cambridge, transporting radioactive material between laboratories. Once he was done with his Ph.D., my father liked to say that he had two job offers: one at the bottom of a salt mine in Ohio. One in Glasgow, in Scotland.

According to my father, people said to him: Don't go to Glasgow! It's too dangerous there!

My father went to Glasgow, where occasionally Glaswegian men who'd had too many pints of lager would try to start fights with him. My father only ever had one pint of lager, at the most, so he'd look at them, bemused.

My father told me that he'd loved Glasgow. In photographs, he wore a lot of tweed and had long sideburns. He was tall and dark and handsome: when Scottish friends told him of the Hogmanay tradition that a home's first visitor in the new year should ideally be a tall and dark-haired man, he was delighted to oblige.

In Glasgow, my father joined a choir. He loved to tell the story of the time he was apprehended by some Glaswegian police on his way home one evening, how they believed him to be a suspicious character, how they demanded that he tell them what was in his bag. Choir music! he said. In

Glasgow, in the building where he lived in a bedsit with a shared bathroom off of Byres Road, my father met my mother, Fiona. She was from Dumfries, a small town a couple of hours south of Glasgow. My mother was working as an educational psychologist, driving her orange Mini around the city to visit schools and homes and hospitals. Before my father, my mother had only had British boyfriends, but she and my father fell in love.

My parents married even though my mother was not Jewish, which some people might have thought would have mattered to my father's family. And my parents married even though some people would have thought that my father being Jewish might have mattered to my mother's family, who attended the Church of Scotland. But the families did not mind. Maybe because my mother was thirty and my father was thirty-two, which were quite old ages for people to be marrying in 1977. Maybe because my grandparents were very kind people.

More than twenty years later, my grandfather, my father's father, told me:

When your dad told me that your mom was not Jewish, the night before their wedding we were sharing a hotel room and he told me in the dark, and I said, 'I know that she's a good one because you picked her.'

I thought this was such a moving story! Such love and acceptance from my grandfather, who did (it was true) adore my mother, and vice versa. But when I repeated this moving story to my father, he snorted (my father had a distinctive snort) and said: That never happened.

As far as I knew, the ways in which my father was Jewish

were mostly food ways: he ate briny fish and cold beet soup from jars. Pumpernickel bagels, grainy dark breads. My father drank little alcohol – Jews don't really drink, he'd say, which was maybe less of a fact than a rumour – and he avoided pork products. When pressed, he claimed it was less a fear of God than a fear of trichinosis. One time, when my brother ordered a pork chop at a restaurant, perhaps to be rebellious, my father sent it back to the kitchen to be cooked again, not once, but twice. I never saw my father send anything else back in a restaurant. At Chanukah my father cooked latkes and sang the Hebrew to bless the menorah, but at Passover he read the English texts.

After they got married my parents moved north of Glasgow, to Aberdeen. My father had a postdoctoral fellowship in medical physics, a post that he acquired in part because Aberdeen was small and remote and cold, which limited the popularity of the opportunity among post-doctoral physicists. My father called it 'winning the scientific lottery'. My mother gave birth to Arthur in the hospital where my father worked. After visiting hours, my father wore his lab coat so that he could pass as a doctor and go to see them. My father joined a camera club and developed his own black-and-white photographs. When my father's fellowship ended, he got a job in Schenectady, in upstate New York: it was a coincidence that it was the town that he'd lived in as a child, where his sister had been born, the last place he'd lived with his parents before his mother got sick. It was a coincidence that he loved. And so, in 1980, my father and my mother and my brother emigrated to America.

In 1981 my parents' second child was born, and that was me. I was born in the same hospital where my grandmother gave birth to my aunt, when my father was four. It was the biggest hospital in Schenectady, and I think it may well have been the same hospital where my grandmother was first treated for cancer. My sister, Elspeth, was born there, too, five years after me.

Twenty-five years after they had moved to America, my father and mother went on a special visit to Aberdeen, for a celebration. I was living in London, then, so I travelled up the country to join them.

What's the celebration for? I asked my father, when I arrived.

Oh, said my father, it's the twenty-fifth anniversary of the time we built the first full-body MRI scanner.

I didn't know you did that, I said, and my father shrugged. I knew that he'd worked on MRI for most of his career, but I did not know that the machine in Aberdeen was the first one to take pictures of whole people. That was what my father meant when he said he'd won the scientific lottery: to work on that project, at that time, in that place.

Is the person who had the first scan invited to the celebration? I asked my father.

No, my father said, we tested it on a patient who was definitely going to die, just in case.

In honour of the celebration there was an article in the city paper, the *Aberdeen Press & Journal*, with a photo of my father in 1979 or 1980, standing by the machine, looking tall and dark and handsome. Inside the machine was his colleague: you could just see the top of his head. The article called my father a 'Scottish scientist' and my father thought that was both funny and wonderful.

My father was not religious, but he had a lot of strong beliefs. When he taught me how to ride a bike when I was five or six years old, he refused to give me training wheels. My father did not believe in training wheels. Instead, he ran behind me as I pedalled down the street in front of our house. He held on to the back of the bike and when he thought I was balanced and ready, he would let go. Several times this caused me to fall over into a hedge on the side of the road. The neighbourhood kids would watch, and cheer. But then one day my father let go and I was just riding.

One evening when I was around that same age and I was telling a long and complex and fictional anecdote at dinner, my father turned to my mother afterwards and said: She is going to scare the heck out of boys.

My father did not tell me that I was pretty. He did not believe in this, either. This was because my father did not like the way that many men his age talked about the intelligence and talents of their sons and the beauty of their daughters.

My father talked about my intelligence and talents all the time and always if I was dressed up for a special occasion then he would take my picture and say that I looked very nice.

My father took a lot of photographs of his kids. He took family photos with his tripod and a timer. He'd arrange us on the sofa in a tableau with a space for him, and then run back to his seat while the timer counted down. When the rolls of film were developed, half of the photos were of his back, of him bending over into his seat while the rest of us smiled our fixed grins at the camera.

(These are some of my favourite photos.)

After my father died, one of his colleagues wrote to me and said that when my father went to radiology conferences to give presentations and discuss the latest breakthroughs in medical imaging he'd say to his friends, distinguished scientists and physicians from around the world: Want to see some great new images? The colleagues would say, Yes, and then my father would pull photographs of his kids out of his pocket.

On Saturday mornings my father made us all oatmeal for breakfast, in a big pot on top of the stove, which I guess was a way of letting my mother sleep in. When I became a teenager and slept later and later my father would still serve up my oatmeal and then when I got down to breakfast at last he would reheat it in the microwave, which was disgusting, but still it was what I had to eat. On Sunday mornings my father made us all pancakes for breakfast, including ones without eggs and milk for my brother, who was allergic to eggs and milk, and including one pancake for the dog.

My father also baked a lot of bread, and once developed a failsafe method for making Jell-O, using the microwave. During the course of its development he produced so much Jell-O, tubs and tubs of it, that he started giving it away to the neighbours. The neighbours seemed a little surprised to receive the gift of Jell-O. My father thought it was a fine gift.

My father was also a person who would always go to visit people he knew when they were in the hospital, even if they were not his closest friends.

When I was a teenager and my father helped me with my math homework he would try to show me special ways to do the math problems, ways that a physicist would do them. They were ways that he described as better or easier, but not ways to do problems that my teachers had taught me at school. Dad, I would say, I don't want to do the math problems this way! Show me how to do them in the normal way! I'm not smart enough to do it this way! and my father would say, You're smart enough, you're just not interested! and we would shout at each other across the kitchen table until one of us would storm away in a huff. It wasn't very nice.

When I was fifteen and had to make a scrapbook of twenty magazine and newspaper articles about chemistry, with captions explaining the meaning, and the night before the scrapbook was due I had written a caption for only one article about chemistry, my father showed me how to use a search engine on the internet for the first time in my life. He stayed up all night with me cutting and pasting and writing explanations about the articles about chemistry. In the morning my father said: Don't do this again, and he drove me to school with my scrapbook.

When I was fourteen and Arthur was seventeen and the brother of the noted home-grown American terrorist the Unabomber was discovered to be living in our quiet and pleasant suburb, my father drove us to his home to join the scrum of journalists so that we could cover the story for the school newspaper.

My father did not really like us to watch television but he would let us read anything. On weekends my father would often take me and Arthur and Elspeth to the library and let us take out any books that we wanted to take out. But when we got home he would make us write them all down in a list on a special form that he printed on the laser printer, with spaces for the due dates, because my father hated paying library fines.

My father would sometimes be sceptical of the speed at which I read my library books and so he would test me by picking one up and opening it to a random page and reading the beginning of a sentence. I would complete the sentence and my father would say that I was amazing. Then he would tell me that I should read *Ivanhoe* (I never read *Ivanhoe*).

When Arthur and Elspeth and I complained that our father had bought us generic Cheerios instead of the superior big-brand ones, my father helped Elspeth to design a project for her school science fair: a double-blind taste test. One evening the family sat around the table and tested Cheerios and Coke and other branded food products against their generic alternatives while Elspeth collected the data, and from that day forth we were never made to eat generic Cheerios again. But we agreed that we all preferred supermarket brand Pop-Tarts.

My father did not really approve of children playing sports with coaches, which he called 'organized sports', because he thought that we should play outside and have a good time, not get yelled at by other kids' dads (my father never volunteered to be the dad who yelled). My father's favourite anecdote of his children's sporting career was of the time my brother joined a local recreational soccer team made up of all the kids whose dads did not want to yell at them. They did not score a single goal all season! my dad liked to recount, to illustrate his point about how organized sports were bad.

Because my dad did not like organized sports, when I was starting high school I decided to join the freshman hockey team as a display of rebellion. My father said it was OK for me to play – he couldn't really stop me, since it was free and also the team was no-cut, no matter how bad you were. But he did say that I had to wear eye protection on the field. Losing your eyesight is very serious, Jean! my father said, and then we got in the car to go shopping for eye protection.

First my father took me to a series of sporting-goods stores to look at squash glasses, and then he said, Oh, I have the solution! He decided that the solution was a pair of glasses from his laboratory with a rubber band, the loop cut, attached to the frames so that they wouldn't fall off.

My father took the afternoon off work to watch the final match of my team's brief, eight-game season. He took photos from the sidelines while I ran up and down a lumpy un-levelled field wearing white knee socks, a plaid kilt and laboratory safety glasses, occasionally whacking at the ball with the j-shaped curve of a varnished wooden stick.

Afterwards, my father hugged me and said, Field hockey is crazy, it's like playing golf while running! and I said, I know, and I think we both knew that this was the conclusion of my career in organized sports, though neither of us said it. But then my father said: It's great that you tried it! and I said, Thanks, Dad, and then he drove me home in his second-hand Mercury Tracer and I felt certain that I was bad at sports but also certain that I was loved.

Around the same time I was playing field hockey, I became catastrophically depressed. Such was the scourge of my depression that I only went to school about half the time, and on many of those days I would cry hysterically for the entire journey from the house to the school in the passenger seat of the car. My father would park the car in the lot of the supermarket that was next to the school and sit with me, facing forward, quietly, until I stopped crying, and then he would sign me in at the school office so that I wouldn't get a detention.

Some mornings he would have to turn around and drive me back home. He did that, too.

When my parents departed my dorm room after dropping me off for the first time at university, in Montreal, after I'd begged them to take me home so that they could enrol me in the local university and they'd said no, my father kissed me and hugged me and then said: Be careful of boys.

My father paid my rent for a month in the summer that I turned twenty-six. I had been living in London for a few years, I had decided to try to change direction in my career, to become a writer. I took a risk and quit my job to do work experience at a national newspaper for a stipend of £50 a week, which was not a very robust income on which to live in London. When discussing the decision with my parents, my father – who had submitted a poem that I'd written about grass to the *New Yorker* when I was fifteen – said he would lend me the money to pay the rent for my room in my apartment that month. This was somewhat humiliating – I was an adult, I felt that I was too old to be an intern – but I was very grateful. For the money, yes, but moreover for the demonstration of belief. (Of course that is a very American thing to say, that my father believed in me, but then that's what I am.)

Some months later, after I'd finished the internship and had a couple of pieces commissioned by big-deal editors, my family attended the wedding of an old family friend, a wedding that was very fancy. The morning after, my father and I strolled with the rest of the family through the sun-drenched corridor of the very fancy wedding hotel on the way to the very fancy post-wedding luncheon. Dad was quiet and thoughtful.

Jean, he said at last, remember the money that you owe me from that time I paid your rent?

Yes, I said. I looked at the very fancy marble floor. I felt guilty that I hadn't mentioned it myself, but the truth was that though I was working again, I could not yet afford to pay him back.

Don't worry about it, my father said.

Wow, I said, thank you, Dad. That's very generous.

You're welcome, he said.

My father smiled.

I smiled.

I'm not getting a wedding, am I? I said.

Nope, he said.

We laughed.

My father and I had similar laughs.

3

My grandfather, my dad's father, died in Chicago in April 2010, which was just a month before his ninety-second birthday, if a month is something that matters when you've lived so many of them. Grandpa told me he was dying, on the phone, which felt preposterous: if he could say those words, *I'm dying*, then it didn't seem like a thing that he should do. It was cancer: what kind didn't matter, the doctors said, because it was already everywhere, and because he was so old. My grandfather did not have Lynch syndrome: his was the kind of cancer that just appears sometimes when cells have been replicating for nine decades. It was the kind of cancer diagnosis that caused people to talk not about fighting battles, but about accepting the inevitable, and celebrating a life well-lived.

My father bought me a flight from London to Chicago. I cried for the first hour or so across the Atlantic, and then I dried my eyes and watched some films. I did not know what would happen next. Other people I'd loved, been close to, had died – my Scottish grandmother, my great-aunt Ruth – but I'd never been present for a death before. The hospice nurse called it 'the dying process'. It was similar to the labour of birth, she explained, a life passage, but with a less happy ending. My brother came from

California, where he'd moved for graduate school. Elspeth came from Edinburgh, where she was working on her Ph.D. Together with our parents, we stayed in a mid-priced motel off the highway somewhere between O'Hare Airport and the apartment that my grandfather shared with his wife. Each morning we gathered in the hotel lobby to eat the complimentary breakfast, and then we drove in a rental car to the low-rise condo where my grandfather had lived my whole life, and where he was now in a hospital bed in the living room, dying.

My grandfather had been a tall and broad and sometimes overweight man, but now he was small. The cancer had moved fast and ravaged him, and we knew that it was almost the end. We gathered, and by we I mean my family and some of the family of my grandfather's second and third wives: after my grandmother, he'd been widowed again, and had stayed close to his second wife's children, as well as the family of his third wife. My grandfather was a man with a very big warm heart, and so there were a lot of other people coming to say goodbye to him, friends of all ages who held him dear. I didn't know who some of those people were and as I watched them file in the door to hold his hand, I felt some resentment towards them and their grief. Some of those people brought potted plants, which struck me as a strange gift for a man who only had a few days to live, though I could see where they were coming from: plants were a thing that my grandfather had always loved.

My grandfather's dying went on for quite a long time: while the hospice nurse made him more comfortable, all there was for the rest of us to do was wait. We stood and sat around the apartment. We held my grandfather's hand. We ate carrot cake and matzo-ball soup and potato pancakes. We helped him drink a little Scotch. Gingerly, we talked about funeral plans: about talking to a rabbi, about catering. My grandfather was going to be buried in the plot next to my grandmother, in a cemetery that my father had never returned to, not in the nearly fifty years since his mother had been put in the ground.

We waited for it to be over, to get back to our regular lives, even though we didn't want it to be over. We had return tickets, and as the day approached, and my grandfather still breathed, we rebooked them. One afternoon in that strange long week, while we were eating the carrot cake, someone noticed that the people with potted plants were somewhat monopolizing my grandfather's limited remaining time on earth. That person said to my father: Do you want us to leave you alone with your dad for a while, so you can have a final conversation? and my father said: Um, not really? because there wasn't a particular thing that he wanted to say, an apology or a declaration or something to confess.

That my father loved my grandfather was not in question, but it was not usually expressed through statements of sentiment. It was in the way that they fought over who'd pick up the check every time they went to dinner. It was in the phone calls that they made to each other during the football games between the colleges that they'd graduated from many decades earlier. It was in the way that they exchanged bone-crushing handshakes every time they met, even in the last five years of my grandfather's life after he had a stroke and spent his days in a wheelchair.

When my grandfather died at last it was at three o'clock in the morning, give or take. He was at home with his wife and his nursing assistant. When we'd left that evening, the hospice nurse had said: It will probably happen tonight, and so I held my grandfather's hand and kissed him goodbye, even though he was on far too much morphine to hear me. We went back to our motel on the side of the highway. In the night, the phone between my bed and my sister's rang and woke me, and I sensed what the news was but answered it anyway: Your grandpa's passed, said the nursing assistant, and I said, Thank you, and I asked him to call my parents' room instead.

The next morning I went to my parents' room down the hall and standing in the doorway I could see my father sitting at the desk, doing something on his laptop. Reading emails, researching funerals. He and my mother had gone to the apartment in the night and watched while my grandfather's body was taken away. My father was not crying, but I looked at him and he looked at me and at that moment I felt that I knew very clearly that even if your parents are very old and have had a rich and well-loved life, if you love them there is never a time in your life when you will feel that you don't want them any more. It was not something that I had ever considered, but at that moment I looked at my father and he looked at me and I knew that there would never be a time in my life when I would regard my parents and think: Yes, I'm ready.

4

My father told me about Lynch syndrome about six months after his father's death. I was back in London; he sent me an email and told me to call him on Skype, which was unlike him. My father emailed everyone in the family almost every day – at least a *New Yorker* cartoon, or a link to an article about terrible Republicans – but it was rare that he initiated a call. My mother was out of town, visiting friends. I wondered if he was just lonely.

I have Lynch syndrome, my father explained, it's a genetic condition that causes cancer.

Earlier that year he'd had a lesion on his chest, so minor that he'd completed the radiation treatment before telling me and my siblings about it. By the way, he'd said, to share that news, I had cancer. I'm fine now.

But the skin cancer, it turned out, was characteristic of Lynch syndrome. So was the cancer that my father's sister, my aunt, had recently been treated for.

My mother must have had it, my father explained, that's why she died so young. It causes colon cancer.

Back in the day, when my grandmother Hannah got sick at thirty-two, it was tragic, but no one knew why it had happened. Not exactly. My father didn't talk about Hannah much. In my bedroom, growing up, I slept under a woollen quilt that she'd knitted and embroidered during one of her long periods of illness. My grandfather didn't talk about her much, either, though sometimes he'd tell me that I looked like her, and she was beautiful (I didn't think I did, but she was).

Sometimes it seemed to me that my grandmother's main family legacy was an excessive, embarrassing preoccupation with healthy bowel movements. Constipation and its cures were discussed with an openness and frequency that I assumed did not occur around the dinner tables of normal families. Dad liked to recount, sometimes in group situations, how he'd conquered this problem when he first moved to Scotland with steel-cut oats. I thought I really had a problem, he'd say, but then I discovered those oats! It was embarrassing, especially when I was a teenager, especially when every family vacation required a detour to an unfamiliar local grocery store so that Dad could source some supplementary fibre.

Hannah was the one who died young, but she was not alone. Her sister, my great-aunt Ruth, had endured a lot of cancer, too, though she lived until her early eighties. At Ruth's funeral, one of my father's cousins remarked that she recalled when Ruth had first called her to say that she had cancer. That phone call had happened thirty years before Ruth died, of bladder cancer. Cancer runs in my mother's family, my father would say, but there was no name for what was running, not until my father and my aunt learned about Lynch syndrome.

Lynch syndrome, Dad said on that Skype call. There's

a fifty per cent chance that you have it, too. You should get tested for it.

OK, Dad, I said, and because I was on camera, I nodded. But I didn't make any plans. It was not a nice thing to think about. I was twenty-nine years old and I was trying to figure out things like: Do I have the right boyfriend? and Do I have the right career? and Will I ever feel strong enough to look at my bank balance when I withdraw money from the cash machine? I did not want to think about the ways in which I might one day die.

Lynch syndrome is a gene mutation. It's a flaw in a cancer-repair gene. It means that instead of repairing themselves from the many uncontrollable things that cause damage, cells become cancerous. It's not rare: more than 1 in 400 people carry it, but they rarely get an early warning, because it's usually diagnosed once people already have cancer, not before. It's found in all kinds of people, but in particular it's found in people who can trace their origins to certain 'founder populations'. Folks who built families with people like them. People from Finland. People from Iceland. French-Canadians. The Amish. Ashkenazi Jews.

Get tested, my father said, and my brother got tested and my sister got tested and my cousin Jennifer, my aunt's only child, got tested. None of them had it.

Get tested, my brother said, the next time I saw him.

Get tested, my sister said, it's easy.

Get tested, my cousin said, I'll come to the doctor with you, if you want me to.

I will, I said.

But I didn't. I didn't get tested because I was sure that I had it.

Sure because of my other inheritances from Dad: childhood asthma, chronic anaemia. We had that similar laugh, and every morning from the time I turned thirty I would look in the mirror first thing and see his features growing into my sleepy face, and I'd rub anti-ageing cream into his lines on my forehead.

How is your father doing? a friend of mine asked, soon after my dad was diagnosed. I was telling the friend about Lynch syndrome, and the test I did not want to have.

He's OK, I said. He's perfectly healthy, although I'm sure it is never nice to learn ahead of time how you are likely to die.

I still did not get tested.

And then, about a year and a half later, Dad told me that he had lung cancer.

When he told me that he had lung cancer that night on Skype in 2012, I was sitting in bed, looking at him and my mother on my laptop. They were next to each other so that both of their faces were framed in the camera. It was late on a Sunday evening for me in London, where I had then been living for nine years, and it was early on a Sunday evening for my parents, because they were at home in Baltimore. They'd moved there from Schenectady in 2007.

I wish I could tell you exactly what my father said because that seems like something that I should remember – maybe I should have written it down, maybe I should have appreciated its significance – but I can't tell you the words he used, not precisely. I just know that two of the words were 'lung cancer' and that my father looked frightened, a kind of fear that I'd never seen before. My mother, too. After my father said 'lung cancer' we ended the call quite quickly, unsure of what else to say. I called my friend Lauren, and cried.

Lung cancer is not a common kind of cancer found in people who have Lynch syndrome, but Lynch syndrome makes every kind of cancer more common. My father never smoked a cigarette, never in his life: it was a fact he insisted on and thought it seemed incredible to me that it had never happened, never ever, not even a puff at a party, my father was a very honest guy. He said that it was because his mother was such a heavy smoker: a two-pack-a-day smoker. He said he remembered spending time with her in their family kitchen, chatting, under a cloud. Maybe that was why my father was never a smoker.

This was something that often felt necessary to say when I told people my father had lung cancer: My father never smoked a cigarette in his life! and every time I said it I felt like I wished I hadn't said it. To say my father had never smoked a cigarette in his life was to imply that he was somehow a better person than other people who had smoked and then died of lung cancer, and of course he was, because he was my father, and of course he was not, because plenty of people get cancer even though they are kind and good. It was not a nice thing to say, and yet: every time I told someone what had happened to my father, I said it.

In the last year of my father's life I started to go home more often. I didn't say that it was because my father was dying, and my parents didn't say it either, but we were always happy to see each other. By then, I was living in Berlin. I'd moved there at the end of 2012 to work as the copywriter at a tech startup that had a lot of money to throw around on travel. My boss agreed to send me on a business trip to New York City once a month under the auspices of work so that I could take the train to Baltimore to see my parents. At first, on these Baltimore visits, we just did our usual things together: went to lunch, went to museums, went to the communist bookstore, watched *The Sopranos*. But as time passed, it got harder. We spent more time at home. On one of my Baltimore trips, we visited the hospital, which is where Dad worked, but also where he was being treated. We sat in a waiting room to see the oncologist. It was large, capacious, plenty of space for dozens of people at various stages in the progression of death. I regarded the people who looked more sick than Dad, and I felt better, and then I felt worse, to have taken comfort in the imminent demise of strangers.

Chronic lung cancer, is what my parents called it when people asked, which sounded better than Stage IV, but was in fact the same thing.

The last time Dad and I ran an errand together, it was November. We went to Staples so that he could get a copy of his Ph.D. thesis in nuclear physics spiral-bound. I didn't ask why, what for. I knew he was dying. We were mostly silent in the car. I said some words about the weather. In the parking lot, Dad unbuckled his seatbelt. The undertone of his complexion had moved from olive to grey. He moved like a cancer patient: slow, pained. He didn't open the door. It felt like when I was a teenager, when we used to sit outside my high school, except now he was the one who did not feel ready to get out of the car.

You know, Dad said, looking ahead through the windshield at the parking lot, which was also grey, you should get the test, for Lynch syndrome.

I will, Dad, I said, I'm working on it.

'I'm working on it' was Dad's signature phrase. He applied it to any situation: choosing the best new household mop. Enfranchising voters. Perfecting a loaf of homemade rye bread. Nuclear physics. 'I'm working on it' meant Dad was thinking about something, considering it. Dad never failed, he just worked on things some more. Everything could always be worked on. In his iPhone 4 he kept lists related to things that he was working on: laboratory experiments. Grant proposals. Movies that he wanted to watch with my mother. One of his lists was entitled 'Bill's cancer'.

Working on it meant that I was thinking about it, too. I was thinking about it a lot. What I didn't explain was that 'I'm working on it' meant that I had decided not to get tested while Dad was alive. I couldn't imagine telling him that I had the thing that was killing him. I thought about telling him that I'd taken the test and it was negative, to put him at ease. But then I thought about having to tell my mother, after Dad died, that I had lied.

I did not get tested.

5

Even if you're not doing it because your father is dying, the age of thirty-two is not a good time to move to New York City for the first time, and neither is the 29th of December. And yet I did just that. I arrived in the city in torrential, freezing rain, with an enormous, dark-green rolling duffel bag that I'd borrowed six years earlier from an ex-boyfriend. I'd promised to return it to him and I hadn't seen him since. It was still marked with gold foiled curling ribbon tied on at some point by his mother so that he wouldn't lose it on his way to graduate school. I left the ribbon on. Every time I saw it coming around a luggage belt at an airport I saw it and remembered what a thoughtful person she was (I really liked that boyfriend's mother, was pretty sad that I lost her in the breakup). When I arrived in New York I had a brand-new deeply discounted Ralph Lauren duvet that I'd acquired from a TJ Maxx in Baltimore, looped in its plastic carrier bag over the handle of my duffle.

Don't let anyone steal that, my mother said, when she saw my burdensome luggage, ready to go in the foyer of my parents' home. I appreciated her belief in me, the value of my modest goods.

My parents took me to the train station with these

bulky items: my mother drove the Subaru, my father came along for the ride. This was the reverse of the usual order of things. I'd noticed it for the first time when they came to pick me up at the Baltimore airport a week or so earlier, my mother with the car keys in her hand. It was Christmas, and my sister and her husband and I had all connected in London on the same transatlantic flight. But where they breezed through, I was slow to emerge from customs. I had imagined it being like the scene in *Closer*, when a customs officer says, 'Welcome home,' to Natalie Portman on her return to New York from London, and she smiles her beautiful enigmatic smile. I imagined saying: I'm back in America after fourteen years away!

I didn't want a song and dance, but a little acknowledgement would have been nice.

Instead, I was pulled out of line by a sweet-faced beagle who caught the scent of the banana that I'd eaten on the plane six hours earlier. The contents of all of my bags were pulled apart and scanned in a giant X-ray machine, exposing that I was not carrying drugs or more bananas, and that I had crumpled the contents of my Berlin life into my bags without organization or folding.

By the time I was allowed to exit into the arrivals hall, my mother was still standing, waiting, with the car keys in her hand, but my father had taken a seat on a bench. No one said anything about this. My parents just hugged me. Before he got sick, my dad had taken pleasure in racing me to the parking lot on airport pickups: his long legs at top speed across the floor while I walked along the moving sidewalk. Now, we all moved at his slow pace. I didn't say anything about it.

Neither did I say anything on the day I persuaded Dad to go for a walk, just a little way down the block. His doctor had told him that despite the pain he was in pretty much all of the time, it was imperative for him to stay on his feet, to keep moving. It was cold, so we put on layers, and then we trudged downhill one step at a time, talking about nothing much at all. We passed the home of a neighbour who had two sons almost precisely the age of my nephews who lived in California. The little neighbour boys were outside playing in their yard, on their swingset, and Dad and I looked at them, and then I looked at Dad, and he didn't say anything, but there were tears streaking his cheeks. I think he knew that he wouldn't see his grandsons again. I looked away, because I did not want to cry as well, and soon after that Dad said he was tired and we turned to go home.

When I arrived in New York I was due to spend my first couple of months in Fort Greene, a pleasant, leafy and gentrified Brooklyn neighbourhood just a single subway stop from Manhattan. But the train deposited me in Penn Station a couple of hours before I was due to meet the estate agent at the apartment, and so I took my suitcase and duvet up the escalators and out of the station – the worst place in New York, and one of the worst places in the world, and a place that hadn't changed at all since I'd first visited it more than twenty years earlier – and headed across Eighth Avenue, through deep, sloshing puddles. I went to a diner, an establishment done up decades earlier in shades of urine. A restaurant with no ambition to be anything but a location for people who want to be somewhere else but can't be. A space to hold bodies that needed to dull liminal pain with carbohydrates and grease.

I was ten years old the first time I came to New York City: in Schenectady, about a hundred and fifty miles up the Hudson River, we spoke of it in hushed tones, with insinuations of danger. There were murders there, and bad things that happened in Central Park: sometimes, my parents hid their copies of *Newsweek* so that we children would not read the details. Everyone knew that if you went to New York City you did not take the subway, and if you did take the subway you did not touch anything.

The things I remember most from that first trip, a day-long jaunt with family friends who were visiting from Scotland, are the Statue of Liberty and the Empire State Building, walking through Macy's, and feeling afraid to touch things, because I understood that I should. I remember riding in a yellow cab with my mother and brother and sister in the back seat, with my father in the front asking the driver about his life before New York, in Russia.

But I also remember going to a diner within a stone's throw of Penn Station, maybe the actual same urine-hued one, in the last hour before our train for home was due to leave. There, I drank a glass of chocolate milk with such enthusiasm – it was something I was not allowed to consume at home, but this was New York City – that the waitress brought me another one. On the house, honey! she said, and her generosity was almost certainly because I looked cute and was well behaved and quiet, but made me feel greedy and embarrassed, for by then I already had come to understand that to be female was to feel ashamed of the public acknowledgement of appetite.

Later, after the meal, we walked through the catacombs of Penn Station to catch our Amtrak home, and passed a man with one leg of his jeans neatly shredded into panels to accommodate the girth of his grotesque swollen calf. The man and I made eye contact and he smiled at me with what looked to me like broad delight, walking with the closest thing to a swagger that kind of leg could permit. The panels of denim swung. For ever after, his smile and his huge calf came to mind whenever someone mentioned New York City. Maybe that's one reason why when so many of the people I went to high school and college with moved down to the city to seek adventure and peril in New York's every day, I had avoided making it my home.

In the urine-coloured diner, at a table for four that felt designed to remind me that I did not have three other people with me, I ordered a turkey burger and French fries. With my glass of water, the waitress brought me two large dill pickles. The pickles made me feel special, until I noticed that the man at the next table also had been given his own pair, alongside his blueberry pancakes. I ate the pickles, which were softer than I would have liked, and stared at the rain and also at my iPhone, willing the clock to move forward to a time when it would be reasonable for me to get in a cab to Brooklyn to meet the man who would give me the keys to my new home. I thought about how, technically, if home is where your stuff is, I lived in the urine-coloured diner.

Isn't it great, I thought, that some day I will reflect on my life on New York and know that everything after the first hour was an improvement?

My bohemian years took place in London, if by bohemian you can mean 'paying the rent with cash advanced from my credit card for an apartment that had no running water three months of the year'. If by bohemian you refer to 'eating oatmeal for breakfast and dinner and also lunch while waiting for a freelance payment'. If by bohemian you mean, when invited to a warehouse party in edgy Hackney Wick, you respond, 'Will we be driving those little forklifts or just, like, carrying flatpacks?'

Arriving in New York for the first time at thirty-two felt like getting to a party and colliding at the entrance with a lot of people who got there before you: you're trying to find space to hang your coat up while they're trying to reclaim theirs, because they're ready to go home. Or move to New Jersey, or to Long Island, or the Bay Area, or in the single most alarming case of leaving New York, to a town of four thousand people in South Dakota that was a three-hour drive from the nearest airport (that's like being at a really good party and leaving it in order to go to an under-attended potluck dinner in a church basement, where everyone has brought the same shop-bought macaroni salad, where everyone is drinking sugar-free grapefruit soda out of wax-coated paper cups).

It's not that these people who were blowing me farewell kisses almost as soon as I arrived thought New York was a bad party. It was a great party, the best ever, they'd had a fabulous time. It was a party that they would be referring to for the rest of their lives – their lives in Long Island or New Jersey or South Dakota – as 'back when I lived in New York'. But they were leaving. They'd had their fill and they were ready to move on.

Behind the people at the door of the party, behind the people who are getting their coats, are the people who are determined to stay until the bitter end. Some of them are the life of the thing, absolutely. You can tell by the way they're dressed that they have money. The party has gone well for them so far. They're sticking around to enjoy what else it has to offer. But some of the people who are still at the party are unravelling around the edges. They've overdone the drugs and booze, or they're feeling pretty bad because at their age it is no longer fun or interesting to be the footloose and fancy-free life of the party. They want someone at the party to take them home, already.

The men you want to meet at the party: well, they seem to have gone quite a while ago, on the arms of women who know the right time to leave a party, women who are a little younger than you, women who might be described as whatever it is that people don't mean when they describe you as 'interesting'.

Women who have very glossy hair.

Some of the late-stayers are more than willing to welcome you to the party – God knows, they are longing for you to inject some new fun and life into this waning affair!

But maybe it is really time for them to go home, to recognize that for them, the party is over. Their dancing is shit, they've run out of things to talk about. They may try to get you to go home with them, but if you do you will find that they live in suffocating apartments, small studios with views of airshafts, or dark wood-panelled rent-controlled places above a grocery store. When these men that you meet at the party lead you to their beds you'll find that they haven't bothered to make them, and in the morning they will offer to make you coffee in a way that means they don't want to make you coffee. If you accept the coffee they don't want to make, the men will talk at you while you drink it about how they should have left the party earlier to go to Los Angeles (and by the party, just to be clear, I mean New York, and by Los Angeles, I mean Los Angeles).

In the beginning, moving to New York at thirty-two felt like going to the kind of party that can make you wish you'd either gotten off your sofa earlier or never left home at all. And yet: here I was.

Then there was the matter of New Year's Eve. I did have some friends in New York: girls from childhood who were now women. People acquired through my time in London who were now, like me, New Yorkers. But everyone still seemed to be away from the city for Christmas, or had plans with their partners. I could have stayed in Baltimore. Should I have stayed in Baltimore? I wondered, as the cab driver dropped me off in the freezing rain a couple of blocks from the apartment, because neither of us knew where it was and we didn't like each other. But I had decided to come to the city because as long as I was in Baltimore I was technically homeless, adrift. I had decided to make my new life in New York. I needed it to begin.

My coworker Melissa was twenty-five, hilarious, beautiful and warm, close enough to graduating from college that she could still start a sentence 'When I was in my sorority' without irony. We'd become friends in Berlin when the company sent her over for two weeks with her new boss to get acquainted with everyone: we drank Aperol spritzes in a square in Mitte on a hot night and shopped for folksy German cardigans in the consignment shop around the corner from the office. When I was twenty-five a woman like Melissa was exactly the kind of confident American that I did not believe I had it in me to be. Melissa was the kind of woman I was hiding from in England. When I was thirty-two, Melissa seemed like someone from whom I could learn how to be an American.

I would have liked to have stayed in on New Year's Eve; if it existed, I would have liked to take some kind of drug that would erase the time between my arrival in New York and the reopening of the office. I had never longed so much to sit at a desk and answer emails, to have a place to go in the morning. But even before I saw my first roach cross the floor of the apartment that I was subletting, where I was sleeping in a pile of clothes and my deeply-discounted Ralph Lauren duvet as I waited for a mattress to be delivered, I knew that spending the night in on my own would not make me feel good. When Melissa posted on Facebook that she and a friend were looking for someone to buy a third ticket to Billy Joel at the Barclays Center on

New Year's Eve, I decided that $300 was a small price to pay to feel that I had a place to go on the dawn of 2014. Even if Billy Joel would also be there.

I met Melissa and her friend Kelly at a restaurant in the East Village before the show. They'd made a reservation for a prix-fixe meal and kindly squeezed me in. I wore a black dress that I'd bought for an office Christmas party a year earlier, did my hair with special care. I took a photo of myself before I left the apartment, because when you are alone on New Year's Eve when you are thirty-two, you have to take a photo of yourself or no one will. And because the occasion seemed like something to record, as if there was a possibility that I'd look back on a photograph and think: Yes, I was happy at the beginning of my life in New York. Or: At least I did my hair with special care.

When I arrived in the restaurant, Melissa and Kelly were wearing black, too: they reminded me of when I was their age, in London, when just a couple of years in it felt like the sprawl of the city might still have a lot of prizes to offer, if I had the tenacity to burrow in and dig them out.

I felt old.

The waiter brought us the prix-fixe menu, and for the thousandth time in my life I said: I'm sorry, but I just need to tell you that I'm allergic to shellfish.

My allergy to shellfish is serious and boring: developed in my mid-twenties, resulting in anaphylactic symptoms and having to have this serious and boring conversation with waiters whenever I'm in a restaurant where shellfish is a risk. Quite often, the news is greeted with weariness, with the assumption that by 'allergy' I mean 'preference', that I am a woman who has a difficult relationship with food.

OK, said the waiter, we won't bring you the amuse bouche, then.

OK, I said, and watched as Melissa and Kelly enjoyed something made out of shrimp. On the menu, the next course was listed as pasta with red snapper. I took a bite. I paused. I chewed and swallowed, because I did not want to be paranoid. I wanted to be polite. I looked at Melissa.

I think, I said.

This has lobster broth in it, she said.

I spat a mouthful into my napkin.

Excuse me, I said.

There was only one toilet in the back of the restaurant so I had to wait for a minute or two before I could push through the door and lock it behind me and commence attempting to make myself throw up. I'm bad at vomiting on command: my gag reflex has always held up fast and brave against the tickle of my index and middle fingers at the back of my throat. So it took some time before I managed to eject the mouthful of fish and pasta and lobster over my hand and into the toilet. I washed my hands and wiped my mouth. I stood at the mirror. My eyes were shot through with the red trails of capillaries that had burst from the pressure of heaving. I dampened a paper towel with cold water. I patted it across my face. I tried to preserve what was left of the make-up I'd applied before I went out.

When I returned to the table, my mouth was tingling, and Melissa was arguing with the waiter.

There was no shellfish in that, he said, I asked the chef, it does not have shellfish. You must have eaten shellfish earlier!

I didn't! I said.

You must have, he said, and then he rolled his eyes.

The restaurant was close and crowded with people trying to make something of the last night of the year. Our table was dead in the centre. It felt like everyone was watching.

Do you think you should go to the ER? Melissa asked.

I would, I said, but I don't have any health insurance until the 1st of January. Tomorrow.

The waiter served us the next course, which I couldn't really contemplate eating.

I'm going to go and buy some Benadryl, I said.

This is how I remember Second Avenue on that night, at that moment: a blast of cold air, black skies, neon lights, me alone on the sidewalk, spinning around as I looked for the sign of a pharmacy or a corner shop. My head pounding from the two glasses of house white wine I'd drunk, and the vomiting.

I found a bodega, I bought some Benadryl, I swallowed it as I walked back down the sidewalk to the restaurant where we paid for our meal despite feeling like we really shouldn't have to, under the circumstances. We took a cab to the stadium in Brooklyn, I sat through the Billy Joel concert, fighting the drowse of antihistamines and early-80s piano tunes. I registered the descent of glitter and balloons when Billy led the stadium in a countdown at midnight.

Afterwards, I said goodnight to Melissa and Kelly – they were going on to another party, one with people their own age, on the Upper East Side. They were kind enough to invite me, but I knew that a thirty-two-year-old rolling on Benadryl was not the companion that they were hoping for, and I walked from the stadium to my sublet apartment (a short distance, but still a silly thing to do on that much Benadryl) and brushed my teeth and went to sleep in my pile on the floor.

In the morning, when I woke, I felt fine. I went into the bathroom and turned on the fluorescent light and said: My face! My beautiful face!

I said it even though no one was there and even though I had never considered my face to be that beautiful. I said it even though the main thing I believed about my face was a thing that my college boyfriend had told me: It's not that pretty, he said, but after a while, I got used to it.

I said it because it seemed like the right thing to say when confronted with a face that was blown up like it belonged to a person who had been defeated in a boxing match. My eyes were narrow slits. My lips beyond bee-stung. I took a photo and texted it to my friend Emily, a doctor.

I'll write you a prescription for an Epipen, she replied.

My face returned to normal by the next day, but I sent the photo of it in its swollen state to the restaurant, requesting a refund. They refused. I sent them the photo I'd taken before I'd gone out that night, to demonstrate that I didn't look like I'd been punched all the time. They refused again. I persisted, and in time the restaurant manager replied and said that I could have a refund, but only on the condition that I came back to the premises to discuss my complaint personally with the chef.

I tried to imagine having that conversation: me versus an angry New Yorker with a range of knives.

I declined.

6

Things improved after New Year's Eve, for those first few weeks of my life in New York. I was lucky: the company that I worked for in Berlin had allowed me to transfer to the New York City office, so the setting of my work changed but my job did not significantly. My New York friends trickled back into town after the holidays, and I made a new one, Joanne, with whom I had many friends in common from London. She was another late arrival to the party, the person who makes you glad you made the effort to show up. I bought black jeans at Uniqlo. I learned that the solid chunks of brown ice at the intersections of wintry sidewalks were most often actually deep puddles. I found a studio where I could practise a particular kind of semi-cultish yoga: I sweated on my purple mat for ninety minutes to pounding trance beats, drank smoothies in the vegan cafe, relished the feeling of freezing sweat on my cheeks when I threw my coat on over my leggings and walked in the snow to the Q train.

Maybe this will be the year I'll learn to stand on my head, I thought, maybe a headstand is the thing that I will accomplish in 2014. I thought about it a lot, like a headstand was a thing that was important.

I experienced novelties, things that all other Americans

knew about but which were unfamiliar to me. To learn more about America, I watched a lot of Netflix, which I had never used before. I liked a show called *Extreme Couponing*, about people who were really good at using coupons, who shopped in giant American discount stores and stored the vast amounts of paper towels and Gatorade and tins of spaghetti that they got for nearly nothing in every nook and cranny in their homes: in basement pantries, in the crawl spaces under their children's beds. *Extreme Couponing* was not the same as *Hoarders*, a show in which acquisition was not celebrated. I did not enjoy *Hoarders* as much.

I sat at bars in the East Village and Williamsburg. I drank wine and ate Brussels sprouts, charred black and covered in big flakes of salt that crunched. They cost $10.

Aren't Brussels sprouts a loathed, disgusting vegetable, not a trendy bar snack? I said.

Where have you been? my friends said.

Europe, I said. I was in Europe.

I said this to friends and I said this to strangers, as if they cared. Baristas in coffee shops, asking me which size of cup I wanted: Gosh, I said, this small cup is so large to me, but then, until recently I lived in Europe. OK, said the baristas, a small then?

Each time I did this I was filled with embarrassment to know myself, but I continued to do it, just as I continued to pronounce my name in the original German, which is not the way that I pronounced it before I lived in Germany. Aydel-SHTINE, I'd say, when people had cause to ask, and they'd say: OK, and how do you spell that? not: Ooh, I can tell you lived in Europe.

One day, on the train to the airport, I found that I did not have enough cash to pay for the ticket, and the man sitting next to me silently handed the conductor a twenty-dollar bill. I told this story again and again as proof of how wonderful America was: And then, I said, I asked the man if I could have his business card so that I could send him a cheque and he waved me away! He did not even want to have sex with me or try to steal my phone! That is what strangers are like in America!

I called my parents on my mobile phone without thinking about the cost or the hour, something I hadn't done in more than a decade. I revelled at being in the same time zone as them. I took the train down to Baltimore for weekends with a white paper bag full of half-moon cookies, because they were my father's childhood favourite. His appetite wasn't great by then, so we cut the half-moons into quarter. By then Dad had been prescribed fentanyl lollipops that seemed to make him a little buzzed but also made him feel a bit better, relieved his terrible pain. Better enough to go to the movies, to eat a half a sandwich in the communist bookstore cafe, to go to an orchestra concert: Dvorak, the New World Symphony. It was good to see my father feeling better, but I also wondered if this meant that my father was now dependent on opiates. I wondered if the fact that no one seemed to be concerned that my father was dependent on opiates was a sign of something even more serious.

Medical marijuana is sort of legal in Maryland, my

mother said one time when we were driving somewhere in the car. I just don't know how to get it.

We can work on that, I said. I imagined doing the research, getting my mother to drive me somewhere in the city in the Subaru to meet a weed dealer, maybe in the bathroom at the communist bookstore, and then going home and getting high with my dad. I had never gotten high before, but imagined it would be fun. I imagined that it would be a thing to look forward to. A thing that I could do.

Four weeks after I moved to New York, at half-past midnight I found myself standing in the hallway outside the apartment where I was staying. The door to the apartment was locked. On the other side of the locked door: my keys, my phone, my wallet, my coat. On the side of the door that I was on: a cruel and strange and unhelpful world, the polar vortex.

My coworker Bob had let me stay in the apartment because he had worn out the amount of time that the co-op board would let him rent the place out. He lived in Los Angeles now, so while he worked on putting the apartment up for sale, he rented it to me, so that I could spend some time figuring out where I really wanted to live in New York.

It's actually against the rules for you to be living there, Bob had explained to me before I moved in. He seemed a little bit afraid of the co-op board.

So if anyone asks who you are, just say that you're my friend and you're helping me to renovate the place for the sale.

Sure, I said.

But ideally, Bob said, try not to talk to anyone.

No problem, I said.

It really was not a problem. I was not there to make friends.

This is how I ended up in the hallway that night: I was doing my laundry in the basement, I was going in and out of the apartment with my laundry. I was in my apartment with my clean laundry – safe! warm! – when I remembered that I hadn't locked the door to the laundry room, and I was sensitive to the importance of not doing anything wrong, of not doing anything to draw attention to the fact that I was living in Bob's apartment. In socked feet I left the apartment to go and lock the laundry room door, overlooking the fact that the laundry room key and the apartment door key were on different key rings. I remembered this fact when the apartment door slammed shut. Of course, this was too late to remember.

I considered my options. I was not wearing shoes, but there was a pair of my boots in the hallway, in a puddle of melted snow and slush, brown with salt. I did have friends in Brooklyn, but I didn't know their addresses. I didn't know their phone numbers, either, of course I didn't. So, I thought, I could pull on my boots and wade to a bodega – coatless, keyless – and beg to use the phone to call a locksmith. But then I'd be locked out of the building altogether. Or, I thought, I could rouse a neighbour – one of the neighbours who I was not supposed to talk to – and ask for help.

I could also cry. But I was disinclined to cry: at that

point, in general. I didn't cry in the urine-coloured diner. I didn't cry when I was rolling on Benadryl. I especially didn't cry when I was sitting in the living room with my dad and he reached for more fentanyl. Crying didn't make things better. It just meant that I had some really big problems, and the additional problem that I was crying.

That's why, when the locksmith turned up, and leaned close to my face, and said, ARE YOU CRYING? I said: No!

(Some neighbours were up, thank goodness, I could hear their television, so I knocked and apologized again and again while the woman lent me a cell phone and the man did the sheepish laugh of a man who had been interrupted by a stranger who'd locked herself out of an apartment while he, the man, was about to have sex. Twenty minutes, said the woman who answered the locksmith hotline, and then I sat on the floor of the hallway by the front door and waited and thought about how I had reached a new nadir in my New York life.)

(At some point, I thought, I will no longer be sitting by this front door and waiting.)

(I tried to focus on that.)

I've been rubbing my eyes, I said to the locksmith, not crying. I'm tired.

And he said, I'm so tired! I would not have come except that you are a lady! My wife is angry that I left her to come here to help you!

And I said, Thanks? and he said, I'm going to try to pick the lock and it will cost $80.

I said, Fine.

The locksmith was exceptionally handsome, with a tool belt and an Israeli accent. Both thick.

You're from Israel? I said, trying to befriend him while he took his pick out, in case that would get me a discount.

Yes, said the locksmith. Well, originally from Uzbekistan.

Tashkent? I said, as if I knew anything about Tashkent.

Yes, said the locksmith.

He tried to pick the lock by poking a pick into it several times in a floppy fashion, as if he'd never seen a lock before.

I can't pick the lock, the locksmith said, so I'm going to drill the lock and that will cost $120.

OK, I said.

He drilled.

I have to replace the lock, said the locksmith. Do you want the expensive good lock or the cheap bad lock?

The cheap bad lock, I said.

OK, said the locksmith. He did some math on a piece of paper.

All together, said the locksmith, that will be $468.

I felt sick. How could I know that he was trying hard enough? I couldn't. He was a lock expert from Tashkent. I was a fucking idiot from America who had locked myself out.

All right, I said. Because there was nothing else I could do.

The locksmith replaced the lock.

I got out my debit card.

If you pay me in cash, said the locksmith, I won't charge you tax.

I don't have $468 in cash, I said to the locksmith.

I'll drive you to an ATM, said the locksmith.

I should not get in this guy's car, I thought, and then I got in his car.

When I first told the story to people I skipped this detail, as it was too upsetting and dangerous and stupid that I got in his car, and then I started thinking that maybe the fact that I survived made it OK that I got in his car, and indeed a kind of important detail, though often when I admitted to people that I got in his car they looked disturbed and uncomfortable as if they wanted to reach back in time and grab my arm with both hands and cry out: JEAN, DO NOT GET IN HIS CAR!

The truth is that I was very alone, and the locksmith had a wedding ring and a photo of a baby as the wallpaper on his phone. The truth is that I got in the locksmith's car.

The locksmith drove me to one ATM, and then I realized that it's not possible to withdraw $468 in one go from an ATM, and then he drove me to another, and then I realized that I was a fool, I had gotten in a car with a man who was driving a car full of locksmith tools.

Take me home, I said, I'll pay with my debit card.

We have to wait for the card to be approved, said the locksmith, it's going to take a while.

He didn't have a credit-card machine. He called someone in Locksmith Central and started reading my card details over the phone.

Now, said the locksmith, we have to wait.

We sat in the car, waiting.

He was silent. I was silent. It was about 3 am.

How do you become a locksmith? I said, to end the uncomfortable silence. Were you just really good at breaking into houses?

The locksmith did not smile.

I laughed. Then I stopped laughing.

Are you Jewish? said the locksmith.

Kind of, I said, I mean, my father is Jewish—

Are you married? said the locksmith. Do you have a boyfriend?

No, I said, I would definitely not be in this situation if I had a boyfriend!

(At that moment I knew, more than I had ever known anything, that if ever I loved a man again, if ever a man loved me, he would always have a set of my keys.)

You should meet my friend! the locksmith said.

Oh? I said.

Yes, said the locksmith, he is a locksmith like me! He's the best. If I was a girl I would totally want to go out with him.

I see, I said.

If he's your boyfriend, said the locksmith, the next time this happens, it will be free.

I don't think I want to go out with your friend, I told the locksmith.

I have your number on the receipt, said the locksmith, as if what I wanted didn't matter, so I'm going to give it to him.

I never heard from the locksmith's friend. I wasn't disappointed by this. Not exactly. After the sting of the $468 passed, I felt happy to have survived the ordeal. Resilient.

7

The sofa was the most extraordinary sofa that I had ever seen. It was covered in black chintz fabric with big flowers all over it in shades of mauve and maroon and pink. The sofa was enormous: it ran up the length of one wall and down another. Sixteen people could have sat on it at least, sixteen people in the throes of the kind of sadness that makes your knees buckle, that makes you disregard the comfort of a sofa, the importance of personal space.

We were in the room with the extraordinary sofa because my father's body was also there: dead, in a cardboard box, which is to say a coffin, but just a temporary one. It was two days after he'd died, and the day after I'd arrived in Baltimore. Arthur had landed on a flight from California that same evening. Elspeth and her husband were on a plane from the UK, and would arrive later that day. But we had to go ahead with making the arrangements, so the three of us – my mother, my brother, me – went to the funeral home.

Do you want to go and view the body? my mother had said, after I arrived in Baltimore, the day after he died, after we had cried together for quite some time. I said, Not really, because I didn't, I did not want my father to be dead at all, but then here we were: my mother, my brother, my dead father and the most extraordinary sofa I had ever seen. Many boxes of Kleenex were distributed on small occasional tables. I guess the funeral home catalogue that sold the extraordinary sofa would also sell those in bulk. I did not want to see my father's dead body. But that morning I'd woken and felt some strange suspicion that if I did not see the body I might feel some kind of regret, an additional one, and so when the funeral director – a squat man in a suit, who was sorry for our loss – opened the door to the room with the sofa and the cardboard box, I stepped inside the room.

In the cardboard box my father looked dead – not a state in which I'd ever seen him, so it was hard to imagine, but also to some extent it met expectations. His eyes were closed as if he was sleeping, but somehow strained, not like when he took naps. He was wearing a hospital gown, and that struck me as inaccurate, because he had arrived at the hospital when he was already dead. Of course it was a matter of convenience: the zip-up cardigan he'd been wearing when he died had been covered in blood. And why would we bring in a shirt or a sweater especially for him to wear in this cardboard box? He was going to be cremated. But I didn't like it, nonetheless. It seemed like in death my father was wearing the jersey for a team that did not deserve his support.

Someone had tidied his hair and face. Not too much; enough. Whatever you do to a body that will soon go up in flames, which was what my father had said that he wanted. We stood there – my mother, my brother and me – and we all cried.

Tranquil Choices was the name of the funeral home. If Dad had been there I thought he would have said, What's the non-tranquil choice? and laughed his distinctive laugh, but he wasn't there, not really. Tranquil Choices was for people like us who had no religious community to fall back on at the worst times of their lives.

Like so many other funeral homes it was a family business. This was a family who had been sorry for your loss for many generations, and maybe that's why after we decided that we had spent enough time with my father's body, which was at once excessive and insufficient, we were led past the extraordinary sofa into a room that looked like the dining room in an old-fashioned family home.

There was a big heavy walnut dining table in the middle, with eight big heavy chairs, and at the end of the room a walnut credenza, the kind of thing that you would display vases on, or family photographs, a soup tureen acquired at a great-aunt's long-ago wedding or even a beloved collection of bowling trophies. But which in this case was being used to display a small range of urns to hold the ashes of a person who you once loved, which the funeral director referred to as 'cremains'.

We sat around the table, the funeral director at the head, which I guess made sense since we no longer had a father.

The funeral director went through a checklist of questions. Did we want a member of the clergy? No, thank you. Did we want a three-hour visitation for a hundred and twenty people with provided drinks and snacks? No, thank you. How did we want to describe Dad in the death notice: did we want to use the word 'beloved'? Or was he 'devoted'? Did we want to have the death notice posted in perpetuity on the funeral home's 'internet website'?

(Everyone knows that websites are on the internet! I wanted to say, but I bit my tongue. It seemed best that I not say anything at all.)

Each time the funeral director offered us another thing that would increase the price of the funeral and my mother said, No, thank you, he would say something like, Oh, you don't want a three-hour visitation for a hundred and twenty people with provided drinks and snacks, or Oh, you don't want a rabbi, in a voice that I took to indicate some doubt that my father was someone who we'd loved very much at all.

Now, said the funeral director, at the end of the check-list, now there will be the matter of an urn for the cremains, and my mother, who was being so astonishing and brave, whose face was set and bright, eyes gleaming with the determination of a woman who was going to get through the worst thing in the world for the sake of her children, said, All right. Mum and Arthur and I all turned to look at the three urns on the credenza, assuming that we'd be choosing from one of them, but then the funeral director stood up and pushed a door open and it turned out that the ones on the credenza were teaser urns. The room next door, as big as the dining room if not bigger, was a funeral boutique. It felt like the time my friend Ian had taken me to our hometown video store, just after our eighteenth birthdays, and said: Are you ready to see something amazing? and then he opened a door that said

'OVER 18' and revealed that next to the hometown video store was a pornographic video store with an inventory twice the size of the regular one.

The funeral boutique was full of all the accessories you'd want to buy for your favourite corpse: urns and coffins, yes, but also prayer books and other religious items for someone to bless and press in their hands. Silk and plastic flowers. Shirt and dress fronts to drape a dead person in so that they don't have to wear a hospital gown in their open casket: for women, a pink dress. For men, a shirt with jacket and tie attached. There were no trousers for sale, I suppose because no one likes to expose the legs of the dead. I looked at the funeral director and thought: Do you ever wonder who you could have been if you hadn't grown up in a family where you were expected one day to run this funeral boutique?

Let's just get the least expensive urn, I said to my mother, because by now I hated the funeral director and wanted to do the thing that he'd find most disappointing.

My mother refused and selected something tasteful and wooden, something that she could display, if she wished, on a dining-room credenza. My mother's own father had died fifty years earlier, when she was sixteen years old. My mother knew what kind of mother her children needed at that time, in that moment.

Back at home, I checked my work email. One colleague had emailed me a selection of photographs of myself: new headshots to use when I did public speaking, or on my LinkedIn profile. On the day of the shoot in the office, several months beforehand in Berlin, they'd hired a make-up artist who put thick make-up on our faces and curled our hair. The photographer had shot us under bright, blown-out lights against a white backdrop. The images were heavily Photoshopped. They weren't great.

What do you think? I said to my mother.

You look like a corpse, she said.

We laughed.

I see what you mean, I said.

Do you want to move back to Berlin? my boss asked, in another email. It was a nice thing for him to ask. I had loved Berlin.

No, thank you, I said to my boss. My life is here now, I said.

And it was. It was there. I just didn't know what 'it', my life in America, was for. I had moved back to America six weeks earlier to be close to my father, and six weeks later he had died.

8

Extending Life was the name of the only magazine in the waiting room of the clinic, and when I sat down to wait for my name to be called I saw it and thought: That's sad. I thought it was sad because I imagined that the people writing and editing *Extending Life* once had big dreams of being journalists on a beat other than end-stage cancer.

I used to be one of them: a young journalist who wrote content for businesses to boost my meagre income from book reviews and op-eds. I covered conference travel and developments in office furniture. I wrote about shipping containers. I edited a website about home improvements for first-time home buyers, filled with articles written by all of my freelance journalist friends who were supplementing their own meagre incomes, people like me who had also never owned or improved a home. In that waiting room I saw *Extending Life* and imagined I knew how the journalists who worked there must have felt every time they slammed out another paragraph about nutritional supplement milkshakes, or detailed how to set up a hospital bed to turn a living room into a dying one.

On that day, in that waiting room, I was not ready to read an issue of *Extending Life*. George Clooney had just gotten married to Amal Alamuddin, and I would have been happy to read the in-depth coverage of their wedding in *People*. I would even have been happy to flick through a decades-old copy of *Cat Fancy*. I was not ready for *Extending Life*, but no other reading material had been provided. The clinic was a place that catered to the very ill, to the dying, but I was not sick. Not yet.

My father had been dead for six months before I was brave enough to go and get the test. I was no longer in a state of deepest grief. I didn't cry every day any more. Just some of them. I spent fewer weekends with my mother in Baltimore and more with my new friends in Brooklyn. I had moved into the apartment that my father was no longer the guarantor for because he was dead, and I had bought a starter sofa, the cheapest on the West Elm website. I hired a man from the internet to assemble my new bed. One morning, I noticed coffee grounds all over the kitchen counter, and then I googled the coffee grounds and I realized that the coffee grounds were mouse shit, and so I also bought a range of different mousetraps, hoping each morning to find dying rodents convulsing in the glue. The traps were always empty.

I went on some dates with men who I met on apps on my phone. I swiped left, and left, and left, and sometimes right. It was a long time since I'd been on a date with an American man, and I wasn't sure that I knew how to do it. On the dates I asked the American men about their lives. Most of the men were quite boring, and most of the time I found that I had forgotten their names by the time we'd bid farewell, me saying: It was nice to meet you! in a tone that probably let them know that it was not. I smiled, I nodded,

I ordered the Brussels sprouts like I'd been doing it my whole life, I split the bill when I knew that I did not want to see them again. Sometimes when the men asked me why I had moved back to America I would tell them about my father, and sometimes I would tell them about my job.

I went to the clinic to see a gastroenterologist. The seats in the clinic were upholstered with chintzy fabric, and the fabric was covered in thick, clear plastic, I guess because gastroenterology patients have a tendency to leak. I slid around on one of the chairs for a few minutes until a nurse took me back to collect my vital statistics.

Any medication? she said.

No, I said.

I see here it says that you were treated for depression, she said, gesturing to the form I filled out in the waiting room with all the details of my medical history since birth.

Yes, I said. When I was a teenager.

Oh, she said. Did you take medication for that?

Yes, I said. But I stopped it about five years ago.

How did it make you feel? the nurse said.

What? I said.

It's a personal question, she said. You see, I've been thinking about taking antidepressants. I've been feeling down.

Oh, I said. Um, I guess they made me feel better?

Oh, OK, said the nurse. You see, I'm a mom and I don't want my little girl to see me so sad all the time.

Yes, I said, I see, of course. You should . . . I mean, I think you should do what's best for you and your daughter.

Thanks, said the nurse.

I felt worried about the nurse.

The nurse showed me into another examination room and left me there for twenty minutes, to wait. I sat on the examination couch, which seemed like the right place to wait, as a patient, even though I was just there to ask the gastroenterologist for a blood test, which was probably something that I could do from a regular chair.

Later that day I was planning to meet Joanne for drinks on a glamorous Manhattan rooftop. I can't recall if it was for a particular occasion or just to celebrate being alive, but that morning I had dressed for it: a nice dress, peep-toe heels, a long necklace. It was an outfit which then felt kind of dumb to be wearing while sitting on an examination couch. My legs dangled.

The room looked like it hadn't been updated since a decade in which I had not yet been born. The sole piece of decoration was a large Proctor & Gamble-branded plastic poster of the human digestive system, rendered in relief. The poster depicted every possible digestive ailment known to man, or at least every possible digestive ailment known to man in the 1970s. Appendicitis and colitis and bowel cancer; stomach cancer and acid reflux. Every organ was sporting a tumour. The medical illustrator had even included a couple of insects, fluttering towards the edge of the poster as if they were trying to escape: parasites.

How are you? said the gastroenterologist when he arrived. He appeared to be only two or three years older than I was.

I'm fine, I said to the gastroenterologist. Even though I've been looking at this horrible poster for twenty minutes.

You'd be surprised, said the gastroenterologist, by how many people there are who don't know what a colon is.

I laughed. He laughed.

How are you . . . feeling? the gastroenterologist said.

Great, I said. I feel great! Except that I need to get tested to see if I have Lynch syndrome.

Right, he said.

My father was diagnosed with it in 2010, I said. He died.

I'm sorry, said the gastroenterologist.

So, I said, I guess I should get tested for it.

Yeah, said the gastroenterologist. OK. I mean, usually I test people for Lynch syndrome by taking a biopsy when they have a colonoscopy.

OK, I said.

But you can have a blood test, said the gastroenterologist. And then if you don't have it you don't have to have a colonoscopy. Do you want a blood test?

Sure, I said.

The gastroenterologist picked up a large book. He started turning pages. A lot of pages.

I guess it's in here somewhere, he said.

Should I google it for you? I said.

No, no, he says. It won't be on the internet! I'm sure it's in this book.

OK, I said. I thought: It's probably on the internet.

I swung my legs a little, like I used to do thirty years earlier, waiting in my paediatrician's office for a physical. I looked at my fancy shoes.

So, said the gastroenterologist, still flipping, your siblings have been tested?

Yes, I said. They're negative. And my cousin on that side of the family was negative, too.

That's great, said the gastroenterologist in a bright voice. So that means . . .

That I still have a fifty per cent chance of having it, I said.

Yeah, said the gastroenterologist, losing his sparkle. Yeah.

It took four weeks to get the results of the test. Once the blood was out of my arm, I didn't think about it again. Instead, I carried on as normal. I went to work in an office on 5th Avenue at my uninspiring and well-paid job that provided me with health insurance. I rode my bike in circles around Prospect Park. I drank iced coffees on patios. I went on some more dates with men whose names I forgot as soon as I said it was nice to meet them.

I went on vacation to Mexico with Joanne, an end-of-summer jaunt, and the gastroenterologist left me a voicemail while we were there. My phone didn't work in Tulum, so I could see that he'd called, but was only able to hear the message a few days after he left it, just after the plane touched down at JFK. I listened as the plane taxied to the gate.

Call me when you can, the gastroenterologist said on the phone, in a voice that sounded relaxed.

Great! I said to Joanne. The gastroenterologist wouldn't just call me on the phone with this terrible life-changing news. I must be negative!

He wouldn't! she said. You must!

It was a nice end to our vacation.

I called the gastroenterologist back the next day.

So, said the gastroenterologist, how was your vacation? You were in Mexico?

It was good, I said, I went to Tulum.

Oh, said the gastroenterologist, did you go snorkelling?

No, I said, yoga.

So, said the gastroenterologist, I'm looking at your test results here, and you do have the mutation for the MSH2 gene that causes Lynch syndrome.

He would. He would just call me on the phone.

Oh, I said.

I'm going to refer you to a geneticist, the gastroenterologist said.

OK, I said.

I said goodbye to the gastroenterologist. I lay down on my bed. I screamed.

Eventually, I picked up my phone. My mother was on a trip to Scotland, visiting Elspeth, and it was too late to call her. So I called Arthur.

I have it, I said.

FUCK, he said.

BEFORE

1

What would you do if you had your whole life ahead of you, if you never thought about how or why you might die?

What I did was follow my heart, or at least what was in my heart when I was not yet twenty-two years old. Which is to say: I followed a boy across the Atlantic. Maybe I didn't follow so much as I pursued. I moved to London to be with Paul in the way that you do when you're that age, and a young woman, and believe that the love you have at not-yet-twenty-two is the greatest love of all. I was also going to graduate school in London, that's true, a good one, but I picked the course because of Paul. Graduate school was a vehicle to get me to London, but in the beginning, Paul was the main reason that I wanted to be there.

The decision was simple. At twenty-one and some months, heart-following seemed like the most important thing for me to do. Other than my heart, I didn't have much: an OK undergraduate degree from McGill University, a group of friends, some vague ambitions to be a writer.

On the last day of my work-study job, as an editorial assistant at the university alumni magazine, my colleagues, who were ten or twenty or thirty years into their careers, took me out to lunch.

What do you want to do now? said one of them, a thirty-something editor.

I took a deep breath. Maybe it was because I'd drunk half a glass of wine at lunch, or maybe it was because I felt close to these people, having spent several hours a week with them in the attic office of the magazine, writing reviews of books by alumni of the university and looking up how much money celebrity graduates had donated (this latter activity was not part of my job, but a hobby). For almost two years we'd drunk the same coffee from the same chipped mugs, and I'd listened to them complain about their spouses or lack thereof.

Well, I said, flattered that the mid-level editor was showing that much interest in my hopes and dreams. Well, eventually I would like to write for the *New Yorker*.

He smirked, or maybe he laughed, I don't remember. I just remember how discouraged I felt when he said, with confidence: That will never happen.

I believed him.

Sometimes, now, I look at people who are ten, fifteen years younger than me, young people who seem to have the wisdom not to follow the whims of romance when they are making decisions about what to do with their lives. I wonder what they know or feel that I didn't.

On the day you left you said you'd only be gone for a year, my mother told me, not long after I returned to America, in the waning days of 2013. She said it with a smile. It was something she recalled with good humour, and it certainly sounded like a thing I might have said on the day I left, which was June 13th, 2003. I remember the date that I left for Ireland so well because it was also my mother's birthday. It also sounded like a thing that my mother, a mother, would have recalled. For a moment I thought about whether her birthday was an inconsiderate day to emigrate, but then I booked the ticket anyway. For what is motherhood but the gradual drifting away of someone that was once part of your own body?

I don't know what it's like to be a mother. Not first-hand. But I do know that once I started approaching the age at which my mother gave birth to me – thirty-four – I began to understand, or maybe, at least, to realize, that my mother's life had not begun on the day that I, or any other of her children, were born.

In the ten years that I spent living on the other side of the Atlantic Ocean from my parents, my mother never asked me to come back to America, or even suggested it. Not even after I called that summer from Berlin and said: I'm thinking about coming home. My mother said, That would be nice, but she did not say, I would like that to happen, or We need you. She did not say the things that parents say in movies. Not telling her adult children how to live their lives is something that my mother has often told me she takes seriously. I appreciate it.

But when I did at last return to America, that December before my father died, my mother still said: You said you'd be back in a year. Perhaps she wanted me to know that she'd noticed. Or maybe she said something similar to her own mother when she left home: when she and my father packed up their home in Scotland, and their small son – my older brother – and left for America. My mother also didn't know how long she'd be away, not for sure. Perhaps it was just one more thing that ran in the family.

Sometimes when I was living so far away from my parents, people I met presumed that I must have made that choice because we didn't get along. That's not the case at all, I'd say. But if the people making the presumption were people who hadn't moved far from home, I don't think they always believed me. And in London, in the south of England, I met many people who had not moved far from home, people who in their twenties and early thirties still saw their parents on a weekly basis, never missed watching a family member blowing out the candles on a birthday cake, had dads who came over to help them build IKEA furniture, had mums who'd pick them up and drive them back home down the motorway to Hampshire or Surrey or East Sussex so that they could sleep in their suburban childhood bedrooms when they had a heavy cold.

If my parents lived in London I would certainly live at home! I'd say, to show that I was not passing judgement on their local lifestyles by living mine in a different way. I meant it. Much as I seemed to have distanced myself from my parents, the truth was I was not rebelling. I was conforming. Some people go to the same universities as their parents, pursue similar careers, marry the kinds of people who their parents are. I was also doing exactly what each of my parents had done, when they were young and had their whole lives ahead of them: crossing the Atlantic to live far away from the people who raised them.

I thought about my parents a lot when I was living in London. But in particular, every now and then, I'd think of my mother when I was on my own and feeling joyful. There were a lot of times in London when I did not feel joyful. Times when I felt like whatever it was I was aiming for by being there was something that I would never be able to get my hands on. In London I so often felt out of place: I like being out of place, I'd think to myself, because that's what I'd chosen to do. But thinking it did not make it true. Not when people interviewing me for jobs told me to go back to America, or when black-cab drivers assumed from my accent that I was a tourist and took too-long routes. Not when the mid-noughties fashion for negging meant that men at parties would introduce themselves to me and then smile and say: Lose your accent.

Every now and then I'd have an evening where I felt OK: like I did the right things, said the right things, laughed the right laugh and wore the right outfit. And sometimes on those right-feeling evenings, when I was on my way home, I would wonder whether in her late twenties, my mother might also have enjoyed the fancy-free feeling of standing on a street corner in the middle of the city where she'd chosen to try out her life as an adult, buzzed from a couple of glasses of wine, and grateful for night air warm enough that she could walk home on her own under bright street lights that made the puddles from afternoon rain flicker.

And then, on the other hand, I also wondered if maybe before she met my father, which didn't happen until she was twenty-nine years old, my mother found it difficult to get to sleep in the solitude of her small apartment because she was wondering if she would ever be normal. If my mother ever also stared at the ceiling above her bed between the hours of two and four a.m. and felt a pain that she could not locate or allay. If my mother ever wondered if she would ever meet a partner and be a mother at all. These were all things that I spent a lot of time thinking about when I was in London, when I wondered if the problem of having my whole life ahead of me, free and clear and open for anything, was that having an unlimited number of options made the chance of choosing the wrong thing so high.

In London, in those long dark nights of staring at the ceiling, I believed that if my life derailed it would be because I made bad decisions that could not be remedied. It never occurred to me that the path of my life was anything but unpredictable, meandering, despite my best attempts to shape and control it. I did not ever consider that my fate was written in every cell of my body. Scripted in the twists of my DNA.

Why do you live in London? people would ask me for the whole time I was there, all of the nine years. It didn't matter that I had a British passport: I still had an American accent, and for that reason I was often regarded as if I had just arrived. Sometimes this was unkind. Sometimes this was well-meaning, people trying to explain to me the way that the government worked, or how to be safe while crossing the road, while I smiled and nodded patiently until they paused for breath, until I could say: I know. I've lived here for almost a decade.

Why are you here? people would say, and sometimes I would say: Because I have a passport! or Because I like it! or Because I can't bear George W. Bush! or maybe even Because it's my home now! But what I didn't say was the truth: I was there because I had once been in love, because I had then been left behind by the person I loved, because I was stubborn. I lived in London because I wanted to be a writer. London seemed liked a good place to do that.

2

I met Paul in Paris, in the spring of 2002, when the city fulfilled its reputation of being a leading destination to fall in love, in that particular season. I was at the end of my third year of university in Montreal; ten days before my departure I had at last ended my relationship with the young man who I had loved throughout most of my undergraduate degree. This relationship had existed somewhat in spite of his best efforts: he'd attempted to break up with me at the end of every semester, only to capitulate each time when I cried.

Somehow I believed that the best thing to do in university, besides getting an education, was to find a husband. My adolescence was spent in a whirl of emotional horror that was eventually calmed by the daily application of Prozac. My psychiatrists, always men, would look at me across their offices, my frowning but composed face, my well-groomed hair, and say things like: It's a chemical imbalance. Because of this, by the time I was in my early twenties, I had come to accept that I was just one of those women who felt too much. I wanted my romantic feelings to have purchase, to feel sure. Perhaps I believed that ticking that particular point on my life's checklist meant that I could focus on the other things in life that interested me.

Perhaps I was not wrong. Perhaps finding a lifelong partner as an undergraduate would have meant I saved many hours of my life that were spent staring at cell phones, willing text messages into existence, or staring across tables at men whose names I could never remember.

I went to Paris for ten days, visiting my friend Lisa, who had been on exchange there all year, studying at Sciences Po. Now when I think about that scenario – I went to Paris for ten days, I slept in a pull-out cot in Lisa's dormitory bedroom right next to her single bed, I caught a terrible cold on the flight over and undoubtedly spent the nights doing all kinds of terrible snoring, TEN DAYS, I feel embarrassed. But I guess that was a normal thing to do with your friends when you were twenty and twenty-two.

And so was falling in love with a boy you met in Paris. We were at Man Ray, a nightclub co-owned by Johnny Depp and John Malkovich – who knew they were even friends? – and that staging of our first encounter sounds very glamorous indeed. But the truth is that Paul was a very gifted and devoted student of political philosophy, on his Erasmus year from his university in Ireland, and I was wearing some black wool boot-cut trousers and a black mohair sweater with a ruffle, my very best sweater from Zara. Along with ten or so other exchange students we sat squashed together on a couple of couches and drank the single drinks that we could each afford on a balcony while below us, rich beautiful French people ate dinner and had cocktails and danced, and we watched them through the railings like opera-goers in the cheap seats, which I suppose, in a way, we were.

Paul winked at me a few nights later, at the end of an evening when we'd boiled pasta with some other students in Lisa's halls of residence during a rainstorm, and by the end of the ten days (TEN DAYS) Lisa and her other friend Adam conspired to leave Paul and me in a bar where all the Sciences Po students went to make out with each other, and then Paul and I made out. We were drinking sangria, he was wearing a red sweater with black stripes, and later I went back with him to his monk-like room in a northerly arrondissement, a development that was probably much appreciated by Lisa as I had already spent NINE NIGHTS sleeping next to her in her tiny room.

Let's save something for later, I said to Paul by way of politely refusing sex, because at twenty I still wasn't all that much in the habit of having sex, and certainly not with strangers, and of course by the morning I was pretty much in love with him, even though I had to sprint to catch my flight and threw up sangria-hued vomit for most of the journey back to Montreal, where I still had to finish my last year at McGill. An email arrived from Paul, and then more emails, and then a February week spent in Dublin where he lived with his family, and then six weeks after I'd finished university my father drove me to Albany International Airport with my two permitted large pieces of luggage and my newly minted British passport, so that I could catch a bus to take me to another airport, a bigger one from which I could actually take a plane, because the international part of Albany International Airport was only in reference to a single flight to Canada. And because moving across an ocean to be with a man when I was not-quite-twenty-two seemed, as much as any of my other options, a reasonable thing to do.

I had a British passport because my mother had me naturalized when I was two years old. In 1981 if you were born to a British father abroad then you were automatically British, and if you were born to a British mother abroad she had to fill out forms to prove that you belonged to her, and should belong to Britain, too. I'd guess it felt quite important to my mother that her children born in America were also from her country. I was a teenager before I learned that these British citizenship rules were the opposite, in a way, to rules of my father's ancestors: that if you're born to a Jewish mother you're Jewish, regardless of who your father is, but if you're born to a Jewish father, distant members of his extended family will occasionally regard you with pity and say things like, Too bad you're not really Jewish. You will go to the bat mitzvahs of cousins but when you turn thirteen no one will tell you that you have become a woman or write you cheques.

(If you're a woman who is married to a man called Edelstein in the 90s in upstate New York, if you change your surname to share his, your child's teacher will ring you up in December to ask you if you'll come in to demonstrate Jewish holiday traditions. If you're my mother you'll pause for a moment and shrug and say: Sure. Why not? And then you'll go in to the school and tell a rapt audience of children about Chanukah. You'll grate potatoes. You'll heat oil. You'll spin dreidels.)

In school, when we learned about immigration, we learned that the people who had come to the United

States – the tired and the poor – were lucky. The United States of America was the greatest country in the world, and our ancestors who had gained admission were the most fortunate people in the world. Because of this education, as a child I always felt a little sorry for everyone who didn't live in America, even though I knew better than many of my classmates that there were other nice places in the world to live.

Every two or three years we went back to Scotland for our summer holidays, where my grandmother lived in a sweet sandstone bungalow in Dumfries and my aunt and uncle and cousins lived in a beautiful house in a smaller town nearby, with sweeping views of the Solway Firth. When we went to Scotland my mother doubled our pocket money and threw out our bed times. At home we drove everywhere but in Scotland we walked up hills and climbed over stiles, picked our way through fields splatted with big wide puddles of cow shit. In Scotland we were sent to the corner shop on our own with a pound coin to buy bread and milk, and when we got a little older, we were allowed to walk in to the town centre by ourselves to buy copies of the *Beano* and sherbet fountains, which we loved not because they were delicious (they were mostly inedible) but because of what Roald Dahl wrote about them in *Boy*. In Scotland we ate hot dinners at lunchtime and banana sandwiches and cake at dinnertime. And on days when it rained in Scotland, which were most days, we were allowed to watch a great deal of television.

In Scotland, life was wonderful and free: the air was fresh, the chips were thick. And yet when we went back to school in America in the autumn, when we returned to our usual lifestyle of driving everywhere in cars and only seeing livestock when we watched our VHS tape of *The Sound of Music*, we would learn about immigrants in history class and I would start feeling sorry for my cousins, who hadn't gotten to come to America, who were trapped in a place where it rained for so many days in the summer and where, in the late 80s, there seemed to be only four television channels and two flavours of ice cream: vanilla, which was sliced from a brick, and rum & raisin, which was disgusting. I understood that the narrative of the American Dream that I learned in my classroom meant that it was right to feel a little bit sorry for anyone who did not live in America, even if they had never shown any inclination of wanting to leave wherever they were from.

My mother was one of the people who had not shown that inclination, not especially: she wasn't a person who'd had a strong ambition to leave the country where she'd grown up. And my father loved Scotland, too. My mother moved to America because my father's career required it, and she moved to a small city where there was no community for expats like her, just a small branch of a club for people of Scottish heritage that didn't admit women, though I believe when she made her enquiries they did say that my father would be welcome to join.

My mother chose to remain on her Green Card. Her document said Resident Alien, and that made us laugh – our mother was an alien! – for twenty years, because my mother was happy to be British. At a mother–daughter Girl Scouts dinner when I was about six, everyone stood to say the Pledge of Allegiance and put their hands over their hearts, the protocol that we'd been taught. Everyone except my mother, and the mother of one of my friends, who was from Tehran. I noticed. Why didn't you say the Pledge? I said to my mother, afterwards, and my mother said: I'm not an American.

I hadn't been taught that it wasn't for everyone.

When my middle-school social-studies teacher asked us to bring in photographs of our immigrant ancestors for display on a bulletin board, my mother laughed a laugh that in hindsight might have been weighed with irony. She gave me one of her with my brother and father in the late 70s, shortly before their emigration. It was a beautiful photo, black and white, in which they were young and smiling and fashionably dressed.

I'm wearing a headscarf like a Russian grandmother, she said, handing me the photo, your teacher will like that.

But in the photo she looked very happy, which was somewhat incongruous with the general aesthetic of the display: hard lives in the old world that allowed us to have good ones in the new.

When my mother did at last become naturalized, more than twenty years after arriving in the United States, it was less because she felt a pull to be part of the greatest country on earth, more because my parents were updating their wills and the lawyer advised it. Furthermore, the laws had changed since my mother's emigration: now, she could become an American without abandoning her British citizenship or saying anything negative about the Queen. She studied hard for the examination, learned facts about American history and culture that I believed I had once learned in school, but couldn't remember why or when or how.

As a pre-teen, shopping for school clothes, my mother refused to buy me fashionable pieces with American flags on them – disrespectful to the flag, she said, although now I wonder if they would have been a little disrespectful to her. But in advance of the occasion of her naturalization, American friends and family showered my mother with an incredible array of American flag-motif gifts, a stream of packages in the mail: umbrellas, stationery, wall hangings, that kind of thing. My mother regarded the gifts with a mixture of gratitude and amusement, and when we went to the courthouse to watch her be sworn in, my mother – then in her mid-fifties – agreed that if called upon to do so, she would bear arms for her new country. In a pew a few feet away, my father and sister and I laughed. We were free to: we were disobedient and nonchalant Americans who were born this way. Americans who had never had to prove their knowledge of the first thirteen states or the name of the first President in order to earn our right to belong.

So I can see why it was important for my mother to make me a British citizen. Unlike my father's people, who had departed from various hostile corners in Europe and the Caucasus on boats in the early part of the twentieth century and even earlier, my mother had not come to America because she was yearning to be free.

Perhaps that's part of why, when I decided to use my privilege to get a British passport so that I could leave my parents behind to follow a boy across the ocean, my mother looked on with approval on the evening when my dad took my passport photo with his digital camera. Get it done at a photo studio? No need, said my father, we'd work on it together. He looked up the parameters on the internet and positioned a piece of white posterboard against the dark wood panelling of the basement for me to stand in front of. In the photo I had shoulder-length curly brown hair that I'd blown out to a frizz, eyebrows plucked so that there was too much space between them. Dad told me to smile, but like most of the immigrant ancestors in our school display, I didn't.

3

Paul was a very nice young man: it seems important to note that, what kind of person that he was, to make it clear that my parents' support of me moving across the Atlantic to be with him was not a crazy thing for them to be doing, or at least not crazy in its entirety. Because although when I say that I met a man in Paris and shared a night of passion with him and as a result decided to move across the Atlantic, it sounds very dramatic and a little bit dangerous, the truth is that Paul's greatest ambition was to be a professor of philosophy. He had a very sweet face and bright blue eyes and prematurely thinning light-brown hair that he wore in a buzz cut close to his scalp, and he wore a wardrobe of clothes that were still for the most part selected by his mother, a lovely woman, with whom, at the time that we met, he still lived (Paul also lived with his father, a lovely man, and his sister, who was also a lovely person).

The plan had been set when I'd visited Dublin during my last Reading Week break from McGill: Paul and I had both been accepted to study at graduate school in London, so I would move to Dublin to spend the summer with him and work until October, when we would move over to London together to start our master's degrees. In Dublin I lived in a shared house, not with Paul, because he still lived with his parents, and also because I felt like it was important for me to maintain some kind of independence. Even though I was far from independent: my parents had bought my plane ticket to Dublin and Paul's mother invited me to dinner with the family six nights out of seven. The room in the Dublin house share was a sublet from a student who was gone for the summer, and the other occupants were another subletter, a nice woman who was studying accountancy, and an older, unsmiling Irish couple – they may have been as old as twenty-eight – for whom the house was their permanent home. The couple regarded me with a coolness that made me think that they saw me as a kind of invasive foreign stranger, which I suppose is exactly what I was. I could hardly blame them for their obvious desire, after a long day at whatever jobs it was that they did, to boil their pasta and eat it off their laps on their sofa while watching reality television.

That was a summer when *Big Brother* was very popular. 'It's 4 p.m. in the Big Brother house,' the narrator would intone in his distinctive northern voice as I crept up and down the stairs, from my room to the kitchen, as if I, too, was being monitored. Such was the unsmiling nature of the couple that I went to great lengths to avoid them, though I don't know what I feared since I already knew they didn't like me. Nonetheless I listened to their movements so that we rarely met. In three months of cohabiting, I set eyes on the woman three times; her partner, only once. I'd fetch my milk and Kellogg's Crunchy Nut cornflakes and carry them back upstairs, where I ate sitting on the floor of my bedroom, leaving white splashes on the carpet that had likely been fitted a decade before.

Milk in Ireland is treated differently from milk in America, less pasteurization, and so on the third or fourth morning I poured the milk on my cornflakes and it came out in solid, clotted, sour chunks. It was unlike anything I had seen before in my whole American life and I recoiled as I would have from a stranger's vomit.

When we'd bought my flight to Ireland my father had insisted on getting a return ticket, not a one-way, that would get me back to America within a month.

Just in case, he said, clicking on the Aer Lingus website. A return ticket is cheaper, my father said, and it also means that you can come home if you're not happy.

I am sure that I rolled my eyes or maybe even said: DAD, because he surely did not know what it was to be not-quite-twenty-two and in love, or at least could not recall. The suggestion that I might want to come home felt insulting. Of course, in retrospect, I know that it is precious: one thing I had in all of my years of living far from my parents was the confidence if all else failed, I could go home.

When I looked at my bowl of ruined milk-chunked cornflakes that morning in Dublin I thought about whether I had known what I was signing up for when I had fallen in love. I thought about the return flight, which was still two weeks in the future, and I thought maybe my dad knew what he was doing when he bought it. But then I got up from the carpet and picked up my bag and went out to catch the 46A bus, to sit on a plaid-upholstered seat on the top deck, to look out the window as the bus wound itself from the Dublin suburbs into the centre of the city, towards O'Connell Bridge and the Millennium Spire, to wonder what my life had become, or would. I was not yet old enough to realize that I'd never really know, that there would never be a time when I could think: *I am here. This is me*, without becoming uncertain again a moment later.

I worked as an office temp that summer. That was what the madness of love had made me do: filing, Dictaphone typing. I had started back home in New York for a few weeks to raise money before my departure. An interview with a beige woman in a windowless office in a business park led to a $10 an hour gig in a windowless office in an allergist's office in a different business park. For eight hours a day I filled out patient intake forms and filed medical notes, which I read, hungry for the intimate details of the lives of strangers.

I read files and drank coffee that was thick with powdered creamer and two sugars and listened to daily updates from one of the medical transcriptionists as she told the other transcriptionists about her baby's chronic constipation.

And then, she said, with triumph, I massaged his anus with castor oil!

On the wall above one of the desks in the office someone had thumbtacked a vivid drawing of Jesus rising from the flames of the burning towers of the World Trade Center, rendered in blue Biro on the back of a pale green sheet of A4 copy paper. Each time I passed by the drawing I felt certain that leaving America was the right thing to do.

In Dublin it would have been more fun to work in a cafe or a restaurant, to pull pints of Guinness in Temple Bar, but I wanted my schedule to align with Paul's, so that we could spend our weekends and evenings together. I signed up at a number of temp agencies, impressed them with my ferocious typing speed but not my completed undergraduate degree, and waited for the calls to come in. I worked as a receptionist at a giant office building, a secretary at an accounting firm, an HR assistant at IBM where I logged the presence and absence of bodies in cubicles.

Sometimes I was spoiled for choice with temp jobs. Sometimes I was not. During one of those times, the not-spoiled, desperate times, I took a job at a mobile-phone company in a business park in Tallaght, which meant that I had to take the bus into the city in order to take another bus out of the city, between ninety minutes and two hours each way, time I spent playing Snake on my Nokia and thinking about what a loser I was. The mobile-phone company was in the process of shutting down and I worked in an open-plan space with a dozen people and as many empty desks, because half of the team had recently been laid off. For this reason it's not surprising that they didn't seem to like me: in part because I'd been brought in to replace their departed colleague, and in part, I suspect, because the boss who had been brought in to 'manage the change' was, like me, an American. Unlike me, the temporary boss was an accomplished body builder, the kind of man whose shoulders and neck had fused into a singular block of spray-tanned muscle. When he entered the room to hushed, strained silence, he'd greet me with warmth; when he departed, the team would start talking again amongst themselves, usually about the horses they were betting on. They didn't ask me if I wanted to bet on the horses, which made me feel like more of an outcast, even though I didn't know anything about horses or betting. It's amazing what will seem interesting when you're outside of a group.

My job in the mobile-phone company was to put sheets of paper in large binders. I guess sometimes I had to punch the holes, and I am sure that I had to put the sheets of paper in some kind of order, but what the order was I don't recall.

One day the American manager came into the room and handed me a large, well-stuffed manila envelope.

Jean, he said smiling, I need you sort out my receipts for me. For my expenses.

Sure thing! I said, with real enthusiasm brought on by the prospect of putting my binders and sheets of paper aside.

The receipts were rolled and folded. I flattened them one by one. Most were from Tesco, or Tesco Express. Some from a moderate-price business hotel. A handful from a chain restaurant that sold roasted meats. The receipts revealed that the American manager had been in Dublin for a couple of months and was staying a short distance from the business park. The receipts also revealed that he consumed dozens of tins of tuna each week, like a beloved, privileged cat. He bought ten or twenty cans at a time. Some regular tuna fish, some tuna steak, but still tinned. With the tuna he ate soy sauce: he bought two bottles of it every week. He also got through a bag or two of jelly babies. And on Sunday, sometimes, he went to the chain restaurant where he ate a Sunday roast and drank one pint of beer.

When I handed the receipts back to the American manager – flattened, stapled in a neat stack – he smiled and said, Thank you, and I smiled and said, You're welcome, but after that I found it hard to look him in the eye, hard to manage the crucial piece of information I knew about him, about how he whiled away lonely nights in his hotel room. As an aspiring writer, I wanted to know the intimate details of strangers' lives, but not this. After I organized the receipts, I'd sit in the room putting my pieces of paper in my binders, while around me the team buzzed their annoyance about the existence of the American manager, about the imminent demise of the company, and I'd think: At least I eat vegetables.

When I got a call for a job working as the receptionist and secretary for Dublin's most important urologist, I was excited. Not because I was interested in urology. I was excited because the job meant that I didn't have to commute to a business park, and I would have unfettered access to people's medical records, which I'd so enjoyed at my first temp job that summer. After spending many hours in high school volunteering in the hospital where I was born, I'd realized that my childhood dream to be a doctor might have been driven more by my interest in people and their life stories rather than my genuine interest in science, not to mention the fact that unexpected views of blood had made me faint on several occasions. When the woman in the temp agency rang to offer me the job, she said: Do you know what a urologist does? and I said, Yes, and she said, Good, which was an ideal way for both of us to avoid saying the word: penis.

The office was across the street from a large hospital, on the ground floor of a Georgian terrace house. In the morning the doctor was in surgery, and it was my job to type his dictated medical notes, yelping occasionally when googling a term to make sure I spelled it right brought up a low-resolution photograph of something sinister or scabbed. At lunch I'd eat a cheese sandwich and then come back to the office to welcome the patients who had appointments with doctors in the afternoon. From my desk I could see right through to the examination room: it was elegant and book-lined, with the table right in the centre, as if the examination would be a performance, or display.

I was conscious that the urologist's office was not a nice place to visit, so I spent a lot of time thinking about how to answer the door in the best way to patients who I assumed would be unhappy to be there. Some days, I experimented: sweeping the door and smiling my brightest American smile, exclaiming WELCOME! to one taken-aback gentleman on the other side of the door. Opening it slowly and mumbling a greeting while staring at my shoes to the next man. After their examinations the patients often had to sit down at the other side of my expansive antique desk to make further appointments. If the outcome of their examinations had been good this was an easy process. If the outcome was not good this was strained and awkward.

One afternoon after I'd worked for the urologist for a few days, he personally escorted a sixty-something patient and his grown-up daughter to my desk. This was not something that he had done before. Please book Mr X for a prostatectomy, he said, and then disappeared back into his examination room, shutting the door. This meant that the man had prostate cancer, I'd worked this out from previous googling, and when he and his daughter sat down at my desk, side by side, they were both crying: not wracking sobs, but with tears sliding down their similar faces.

All right, I said, realizing that everything I thought I knew about being efficient and friendly was now irrelevant. My eyes filled up with tears as I went down the checklist with them: name, date of birth, calling the hospital to confirm the timing, here's your list of pre-operative requirements, nil by mouth. I tried to tell them these important things in a way that seemed professional but of course this was impossible because I was crying while I did it, though they were kind enough to pretend I wasn't, I suppose in the way that I pretended they weren't crying, either. I cried and they cried and we all helped each other get to the end of the process, and then they got up to leave. I don't know what I said to them. Goodbye? Good luck? Maybe I just tried to smile. I wiped my eyes with the back of my hand and felt I understood right then, right there, for the first time in my life, the kind of fear that cancer makes people fear.

I wondered for a while afterwards what became of them, of him, but of course I never found out. I wondered whether I was present for one of the most altering events in their lives, if that was the beginning of that man's end, or if in years to come they would tell the story of the diagnosis and say: And there was this American girl there, making the appointment, and she was crying! But it wasn't a big deal at all, was it, Dad?

As I recall, Paul and I only fought twice that summer: once when I suggested that instead of panicking about his upcoming driving test, he could feel confident that he had a girlfriend who already had a licence. Once when he tried to get me to go into deep water in the Irish Sea, at the icy spot in Dun Laoghaire harbour where plump Buck Mulligan went for his swim. Aside from that, Paul made me very happy, and I him. We moved to London together, we studied for our master's degrees, we drank many pints of alcohol, made friends with other international students, complained about our common penury. We went on vacations to Spain where we mostly stayed still on sunloungers, transforming our bodies from Celtic and pale to shades of mahogany. I moved into a shared house in Clapham with Paul's sister and her boyfriend and another flatmate. We drank cups of tea and cooked each other lavish dinners on rotation. I got a job at the pub in Clapham Junction train station, came home after shifts covered in handprint bruises from the clientele who grabbed and prodded me as I moved through their throngs to deliver hot chips and chicken sandwiches. I showed Paul the handprints and we accepted that they weren't very nice, but were part of the job. Discussing our future, Paul and I agreed we'd stay in London for a year after we finished our degrees – this was the easiest way for us to stay together, because we both had EU passports and he did not have an American one – and then we'd move to the US together, New York or Boston, him to do his Ph.D., me to pursue my career in book publishing.

Paul went to Brussels in the autumn after we finished at the LSE, to do an internship. I stayed back in London, worked as a waitress, and applied for jobs. Most days I spent slumped on the sofa in the rented house in Clapham, waiting for my shifts, refreshing my email for news of job applications, watching music videos and the worst of low-budget reality shows on MTV: *Room Raiders*, a sort of blind-dating show where the contestants pre-screened other contestants for romance by digging through the contents of their bedrooms, scanning sheets with a blacklight for signs of cum. I don't know if it was depression, or just acceptance, that led me to come to understand this was my life now: poor posture, satellite television, serving expensive once-frozen hamburgers to rich English people who drank too much at lunch. Paul and I spoke on the phone every night: he told me about all the fun he was having with his Brussels flatmates (four girls) and all the frites he was eating. He told me that he missed me, cried about it sometimes, but it was difficult for me not to feel hard done by when he was having a great adventure. I saw the rest of my life strung before me as beads on a necklace, each bead representing another episode of *Room Raiders*. After a while I'd seen all of the episodes, but when they aired again, I watched them, too, even though I already knew where the cum was.

Of course we didn't stay together. Paul won a Fulbright

scholarship and wanted to use it to go to study in Boston. By then, I'd gotten an internship in a literary agency, and didn't want to give up the small purchases I'd clawed in the industry that I so desperately wanted to work in. Two years earlier I had believed that emigrating for a man was a good idea, but now, with the slightest taste of what it was to do work that I found meaningful, I resisted the call to do it again. Paul came back to London from Brussels for one final weekend to try to work it out. It was a Bank Holiday, so we spent three days arguing and crying and then going on pleasant outings. On our last day together we rode a tandem bicycle through Battersea Park, because I had always wanted to ride a tandem bicycle. When I was sitting in the front and steering, we rode for miles: straight and true. When Paul took the front seat, we fell off, again and again. The next morning we both sobbed while he left. We were finished. Maybe the bicycle was a metaphor for something. Maybe it wasn't.

A few weeks later I was offered a job in publishing in New York City, working as the assistant to a literary scout. Maybe the distance between New York and Boston was one that could be overcome. I wrote an email to Paul and told him about the offer, that I had the chance of moving back to America, and then I turned it down. Even though I didn't have another job in London lined up. Even though being without him felt, in some ways, like a kind of torture.

One day, I told people, again and again – my friends, my parents, the people who didn't understand my decision, or at least seemed surprised by it – one day I know that I'll wake up and know that I'm ready to go back to America, and then I'll go. That's what I said: One day. Not now. Sometimes when people asked me why I lived in London, I'd think: Because I'm trying to prove a point to someone who left me behind. But I never said it out loud.

4

You couldn't stand up in the shower in the flat on Cephas Street. Lisa and I figured that out when we viewed the place the first time. The showers were tucked in the eaves of the roof and to use them you'd have to sit on the cold porcelain of the bathtub. But it was London in 2005 and we had our first jobs with pay cheques that came once a month, so of course this flat – renovated recently, with fresh cream carpets – seemed like a dream come true. Two years in London had helped me to understand that Americans had unreasonable expectations of cleanliness, of comfort. Before we moved into the flat on Cephas Street I'd lived for a summer in a house on top of a hill in Archway that was so thick with the filth of generations of flat-sharing inhabitants that everything I owned became covered in grease: my dresses, my books, my face. I'd not had problems with acne since my teenage years, and then only mild, but when my parents came to visit when I lived in that oily home and they beheld the state of my forehead and cheeks and chin, my mother, who rarely commented on my appearance unless I'd made an obvious effort, made the unprecedented suggestion that I should go to see a dermatologist.

So I moved out of the house of grease into the flat on

Cephas Street with Lisa, the friend from Montreal who I'd visited in Paris and who was now working in her first full-time job after completing her own master's degree. Cephas Street was in East London, on the southern edge of Bethnal Green, and the flat was in a converted church: it had been built in the early nineteenth century, along with rows and rows of terraced houses for working-class people making their way in London. Bombing in the Second World War had mostly put paid to the terraces, but the church had remained as stacks of square council estates had been built up around it. There was still a cross on the top of the steeple, but below there were twenty-eight apartments containing an assortment of young professionals. When people came over they'd remark on how the churchyard had been paved over, to put up a parking lot. Wouldn't it have once been a graveyard for the parishioners? they asked. I chose not to consider it.

The commute was pretty easy: forty-five minutes or so straight to Marble Arch from Bethnal Green tube station, where a plaque on the entrance that I used reminded me each morning that it had been the site of the greatest number of simultaneous deaths in the history of the Blitz. It was a little while before I learned that the deaths happened not because a bomb fell in that spot, but because people descending the stairs to take cover from what they thought was an attack, but which was actually weapons testing, trampled each other to death.

I still wanted to be a writer. I think that was what I had always wanted: I'd professed interest at different times in medicine, psychology, politics. I'd been lucky to have had the kind of education that meant all of these things would have been possible at one time or another, but the truth was that all I wanted to do was write.

And yet: I also didn't believe that I could write. Not for a living, not really. At twenty-three or twenty-four I believed that if I was really going to be a writer it would have happened already. That it hadn't surely meant that I lacked the talent. In my interviews for publishing jobs, I said: I used to want to be a writer, but I know I'm not good enough, so I want to work with people who do have the talent! People hiring for entry-level publishing jobs seemed to like that expression of low self-esteem.

My job, the first one with the real monthly pay cheque, was at a literary agency in Marylebone, working as the assistant to a woman who was well known in the industry for striking great deals for her famous clients, and less well known for not being very kind to her long-suffering assistants.

Young people at the competing agency where I was interning before I got the job exchanged glances with each other when I told them I'd accepted the role. Don't do it, one or two of them said, people who were friends with the assistant who I was replacing, it's not a good idea to work for her.

These people have no idea who I am, I thought to myself, I am Jean Hannah Edelstein, young American woman! There is nothing that I can't achieve with my pluck and sass. For while I was not assured of my skills as a writer, I was certain that I was good at reading, and drinking coffee, and wearing tweed, which was how I believed people working in publishing spent much of their time.

Also, I was desperate for a proper job. I had no problem getting interviews for jobs in publishing, but I seemed to have a lot of trouble getting offers. Once, two rejections in one day for the same role at two different companies. One said I did not have enough experience; the other called me overqualified. To make ends meet, I got a side job ghost-writing a book about hair colour for a tiny publishing company run by a divorced Eastern European countess and her new husband, a once-notorious armed robber. When the woman everyone told me not to work for offered me a job, I was ecstatic: finally, I could start my real life.

Being an assistant to a literary agent meant being her secretary: at some point in time I guess someone had decided that the bright young educated things who were hired for the job with dreams of becoming agents themselves wouldn't like to be called secretaries, but that's what we were. We typed and filed and made restaurant reservations for long lunches, and if our bosses left their coats behind in the restaurants because they'd drunk a bit too much at the lunches, we retraced their steps to find and reunite the coats with their owners. In my final interview before I got the job offer, the MD of the company looked at me coolly across the room and said, There's no space for advancement here, and I smiled back at him and said: That's fine with me! because by then I had learned that my American-style ambition was not welcome in this old-fashioned English industry. A few weeks after I joined the company that same MD was sacked from his job. We were summoned on his last Friday to toast his involuntary departure with champagne that was poured into glasses arranged attractively on top of a vast filing cabinet. I'm not sure this is normal? I whispered to one of the other glorified secretaries as we sipped our drinks, and she shrugged.

At the agency I sat in a cubicle with the other assistants in an open-plan windowless section at the centre of the office. Our bosses, the agents, had their own separate offices around the perimeter of the building, where they took meetings, drank tea, marked up writing. One of them even smoked. In the space between our cubicles and the perimeter offices was a half-wall constructed of heavy metal filing cabinets that stretched down the length of the office, in which it was our job to file every piece of correspondence that came and went, including the emails. It was our job to print those and then to take the paper copies of the emails and put them in the vast filing cabinets. I didn't really like to file the hard copies of the emails, because I thought it was stupid to print them out, and I've never been very good at doing things I find stupid. I thought perhaps it should have been sufficient, more than, for us to keep digital copies. And now that I look back, if I'm honest with myself, I can acknowledge that maybe part of the reason that I was not very good at this job was that I often just did not file the hard copies of the emails. Sometimes I didn't print them at all, or sometimes I printed them and then filed them in the secure recycling bin, or under a stack of books on my desk.

I was issued with a Dictaphone on my first day of work, and a handful of cassette tapes. It was 2005 but still I was expected to use a Dictaphone, so it was lucky that I'd honed my skills in the office of the penis doctor. The agent I worked for would sit at her desk in her office across from my desk and I would watch her speak into the Dictaphone and brace myself for when she crossed out of her office and leaned over the edge of my cubicle and handed me a tape. Here you go, Jean, she would say, do you have any fresh tapes? and I'd have to hand back the ones that I'd rewound for her to re-use, maybe because you couldn't really buy them any more, because it was 2005.

Every morning it was my job to go into my boss's office and delete all of the spam emails from her inbox before she got in, maybe because she was too grand to deign to look at spam email, and maybe because – so rumour had it – she had engaged in a long correspondence with an 'African prince' who had recently suffered the loss of a wealthy and elderly relative.

My boss had a distinctive voice, it carried far, and for that reason there were many complaints about the way that she spoke to me. When disappointed in me, which was most of the time, she'd cry out, OH, JEAN, across the room, and I'd go scurrying through to see what I had done wrong, which was everything on days when she was in a bad mood, and nothing on days when she was feeling happy and relaxed. On the rarest of these days, the most happy and relaxed ones, she'd take me to lunch in the fancy restaurants in Covent Garden where dealmakers made deals and left behind coats.

In the restaurants, we'd drink negronis – she'd order them, we'd never have fewer than two – and then she would tell me more than I would have liked about her life outside of work, which is to say anything at all. I think this is what made her feel close to me: I think this is probably how she treated all of the people who she employed to work for her, which was quite a few people.

Maybe this close feeling was why, on one of the days when she was in a good mood, the boss invited me to a fancy publishing party. I wasn't getting paid very much and the party sounded like it would have good canapés, so I went. When at that party my boss asked me, in a group of people, if I would promise to ensure that she had a partic- ular kind of ham at her funeral, if I would make sure to get some special ham from one of the restaurants where I made the reservations, as if funeral catering was the responsibility of a literary agent's assistant, I said yes. Yes, I will organize the ham at your funeral.

After all, I had never had a real job before, and as such I understood that what I was experiencing was simply the nature of having a job, that having a job involved saying yes to whatever your boss wanted, and to being shouted at.

Here are some things that my boss shouted at me about in her distinctive voice:

When I brought her a lunch that she claimed to be allergic to, although I'd asked her beforehand if she had any allergies.

When she didn't like the end of a manuscript that an author had submitted. On that occasion she accused me of failing to print the whole thing for her; and when I advised that was, in fact, the end, she said, in a bad-tempered tone: Well, it's very abrupt!

She also shouted at me when I discovered that the previous assistant, no doubt in an act of rebellion, had ignored a large payment due to a writer that was now outstanding for three months.

She shouted when she dug through the piles on my desk when I went on vacation and discovered that I had not filed all of the printed-out emails.

She shouted at me when a book that a writer had sent to her was sold by another agent to a publisher for a great deal of money, a book that she hadn't read because she thought it was too long, and had dumped the box it came in – she was right, it was too long – on my desk. It made her angry, somehow, that I hadn't identified that the book would be a critical success, that I hadn't carried the reams of paper back and forth from my desk to hers during our morning meetings until she agreed to read them. You need to know what I'm thinking before I think it! she told me during one of the worst times, one of the occasions when she shouted so much that I started crying.

There was no one to help me in the company, not really: my fellow assistants were kind to me, and the office manager listened to my woes, but none of the people who had the power to make anything better for me did anything to make it better. For the most part the extent of the powerful people's acknowledgement of my existence was to leave Jewish-themed books and magazines on my desk: I thought this would interest you, one said, pressing a novel into my hands that was about a Hasidic woman, as if she believed that was a way for me to feel seen.

Maybe it would be better if you were a boy, another colleague remarked in a thoughtful tone, when I appealed to him for advice on how to navigate the situation.

At night in the flat on Cephas Street, I would wake often and stare out the skylight in the slanted ceiling above my bed, at the glowing and starless London sky. I'd lie there and think about invoices, about writers who hadn't delivered their manuscripts on time, about publishers who hadn't paid their writers, of hard copies of emails that I had not filed, about the distinctive voice. OH, JEAN, I'd hear, OH, JEAN. OH, JEAN. And then I'd wonder whether I had made the right decision to stay in London, after all. I'd wonder if the job was some kind of karmic punishment.

Sometimes Paul and I emailed each other, fragile words of apology and acceptance, and then at Christmas, when I went back to America to see my family, I saw Paul, too. We kissed, and I thought we might get back together, and then after one particularly bad run of days at work I wrote to him: Should I move to Boston? I will. He responded, a few days later: No. Don't.

Whatever part of my heart that had healed was broken again.

Each Monday a tremendous bouquet of flowers was delivered to the company to decorate the reception desk at the front of the office, and each Friday the office manager would run a raffle to select who would be given the flowers – a little wilted, but still abundant and lovely – to take home. The office manager would send an email round the office and if you were a person who would like the flowers to brighten your depressing London apartment with limited running water, you could email her back to have your name put in the hat. When things got especially bad for me, when the people who sat on the floor below my desk started remarking that even they could hear what was going on above them, the office manager started picking me as the winner for the flowers most of the time. Jean wins again! she'd write in an all-office email, and everyone else would smile and nod, as if I was lucky, instead of the opposite of that.

The office manager would wrap the dripping stems of the flowers in a plastic bag and hand them to me with an expression that resembled a smile but acknowledged that the situation was really about pain. I'd lug the flowers home on the tube, clutching them to my chest as if I was on my way to a funeral for my happiness, smudging indelible orange pollen from lily stamens into my navy trench coat. One Friday I felt so bad that I couldn't bear to bring the flowers into my flat, to have them all weekend as a fragrant reminder of my failure, so as I walked towards Cephas Street I ripped the plastic bag off the stems and stashed the flowers up high in a tree. To rot, or maybe to bring pleasure to someone who knew how to experience that.

Mark was a friend of a colleague at my horrible job, and when my colleague decided to set us up on a blind date I think it was partly because she thought we'd get along, and partly because she wanted to do something to make me look less mournful as I sat at my desk, rewinding and fast-forwarding the Dictaphone tapes, trying not to cry. Mark and I met the first time at Tate Britain and I immediately thought he was wonderful: he was sitting on the front steps, reading the *New Yorker* with nonchalance, or a careful performance of it. I thought he looked ideal. It took a few more encounters for me to notice that he also looked exactly like my father.

The breakup with Paul devastated me, but I never thought it would lead to a long period of being alone. Before him I'd been in two long relationships, as much as relationships can be a thing when you're sixteen and your boyfriend is fifteen and neither of you has a driver's licence. When Paul and I had broken up I was wretched, but I also assumed that his replacement would swim into vision within a matter of weeks, because that's what I was used to. But that is not what happened. After Paul, before Mark, I'd dated a few men with unsatisfactory results, which I measured in terms of their lack of interest in long-term relationships with me, not really accounting for my interest in long-term relationships with them. I was waiting to be chosen, not to choose.

Mark was sophisticated, which is to say that he was thirty-one years old, which was old enough to remember a substantial amount of the 1970s, a decade in which I had not been alive. Mark owned an apartment in Kensal Rise that he lived in with a friend of his from college, had a job as a consultant where he had responsibilities above and beyond getting shouted at. Mark had gone to a fancy university, fancier than mine, one that he mentioned by name every time we met, even though he had graduated from it nearly a decade before. Until recently he had been in a rock band that he assured me had been on the verge of tremendous fame before there had been some kind of a fissure brought on by someone's girlfriend. Mark compared the girlfriend to Yoko Ono. He carried his Tate membership card in his wallet and owned a part-share in a racing greyhound, even though, or maybe because, he didn't like dogs. Each time Mark and I slept together the first thing he would say to me, in the post-coital glow, was: Thank you. He said it with real warmth and gratitude, as if he was full of genuine polite appreciation for my contribution to the experience. It was an expression of thanks that was not inappropriate, per se, but also would not have been inappropriate if I had made him a very nice casserole. 'Thank you' was not what I wanted to hear, but I took it. Mark was English, after all, and in three years of living in his country I had come to understand that the English were not explicit about how they felt.

My life at work that autumn continued to be terrible. My boss continued to lose her temper and I continued to hide more swathes of printed-out emails in my desk, stuffing them into a drawer that I locked so that she could not find them, like a shameful stash of cocaine. I was not allowed my own space at work, and so I decided to take it. Rifling through my desk was now of her favourite occupations: I'd see her hovering there when I entered the floor, from the other end of the room, and my heart would drop into my stomach. But for those few weeks when Mark was around, I stopped minding the rifling quite so much, because he would email me once a day and sign each correspondence with three kisses. Maybe, I thought to myself, it's unrealistic to think that everything in my life should be good all at once. Maybe I don't need to worry so much about how much I hate my job, or how the career for which I studied and worked so hard is going nowhere. Not when I have this really nice boyfriend. Maybe I was right to stay in London after all.

I have a new boyfriend, I told my parents on one of our weekly phone calls, even though Mark had never called himself my boyfriend, even though I would not have dared to say that to his face, because I knew, just like all of my friends knew, that the worst possible thing you could do with a man you were dating was to express a personal preference. We talked about this, my girlfriends and I, over bottles of house white wine: someone would tell us a story of how she had been wronged, of how a man had denied her request for a little bit of time, attention, or respect, and we'd shake our heads with pity but also understanding of how the young woman in question had fatally erred: by wanting something, by asking for it.

I dared not do such a thing with Mark. I accepted his choices of restaurants, of films, of not holding my hand when we were out in public, but I believed that he was my boyfriend: the symptoms were present. We were seeing each other a couple of times a week, we were texting each other on nights apart with our Nokia phones, we were having the kind of sex that I didn't believe you could have with more than one person in a month. What does he look like? my mother said, and I laughed and said, Well, I guess he kind of looks like Dad! and then I didn't really think about that again until a few days later when my father sent me an email, with the subject line: Picture.

In the email was a diptych he had created: a photo of Mark that he'd found on MySpace. A photo of him, at a similar age, wearing a similar hat. They looked nearly identical. I was sitting at work when I got the email, in my cubicle, and it was so shocking that I climbed out of my rolling desk chair and lay down on the carpet.

I showed the diptych to my friends. Why are you showing me a photo of Mark and his father? they said, or in some cases, they said: This is so creepy! When is Dad coming over? my flatmate said. I met him on a blind date, I told people. It would be awful if I had picked him out of a room myself but it's not my fault.

At last I decided I had to tell Mark about it, one night as we were falling asleep.

So, I said, I have to tell you something. You really look a lot like my dad.

For a moment he was silent. Oh, Mark said, at last, I guess that's creepy for you.

That Mark and my boss broke up with me on the same day was just a coincidence, I'm sure. It was a couple of weeks before Christmas, and a couple of years before the financial crisis, which meant that everyone in publishing was out every night, drinking excessive amounts of mulled wine. My boss came in that morning with a look on her face that made me think she probably had a hangover – she'd been out at one of those parties the night before, I'd seen it in her calendar – and as she approached my whole body stiffened, in the way that a body stiffens when it's preparing to receive a punch. She rifled through the pile of books and papers on her desk and then came through to ask me where one item was.

Oh, I said, you asked me to give it to the accounts department, so it's on the accountant's desk. But I can make you a photocopy right now, it will just take a minute.

What the hell is wrong with you? my boss said. Are you crazy?

I was sitting down at my desk. She was leaning over the edge of the cubicle, glaring down at me. I swallowed.

I don't think it's fair for you to speak to me this way, I said, in a voice that was meant to sound strong but instead sounded weak, and shaky.

Jean! she said. Come in to my office!

I followed, and then she told me that the time had come for me to find a new job.

The other thing that I remember from that day is someone telling me, helpfully, that if you drink a glass of water you can't cry at the same time.

Later that evening, after a meal and a lot of wine at Pizza Express with one of my friends from the office, I saw that I had a missed call from Mark. We had never spoken on the phone before, so I knew it wasn't good. I also remembered the previous Sunday morning, when he'd kissed me goodbye as I was leaving his house and yet I felt not embraced, but dismissed.

How are you? Mark said on the phone, and I said, Well, I got fired today, and he said: Oh. Well. I'm sorry.

And I said: Yup.

And he said: I'm sorry, but I don't think we can see each other any more.

I persuaded him to come over to talk to me in person, I don't know why, except perhaps that I already felt hurt and alone, would rather process the information in the company of another warm body, even if it was a body that didn't care for me. Mark sat opposite to me on the sofa and explained, slowly and carefully, as if I was a child and he was my thirty-one-year-old father, that sometimes two people can have great sex but aren't meant to be a couple. It was patronizing but also: it was a lesson I had not yet learned, and one that he, older than me by seven years, evidently knew deep in his heart.

My time with Mark was brief, would be outlasted in years to come by other men who didn't care for me a great deal. The same goes for the boss who told me that I should find another job that day. I've had so many bosses since: some good, some terrible in other ways. But these two people both stand out as the first who made me feel that I had overestimated my value.

At least only one day of my life is ruined! I said to Mark, in reference to the double rejection, and when he at last left, with references to future friendship that we both knew would never be fulfilled, I sat down in the shower – because I was sad but also because it wasn't possible to stand up in the shower in the flat on Cephas Street – and cried. At that time of year, when the cold air outside froze the pipes, it was easy for tears to flow faster than the water from the taps.

I was due to travel home to upstate New York a couple of weeks later, to spend the Christmas break. It was the last Christmas we'd have in the home my siblings and I grew up in: my parents were putting it on the market, to move to Baltimore, for my father's new job. But in the days that followed my firing and dumping I decided not to go. If I sat on my parents' sofa, I believed, I would never get up again, and my whole small life that I'd built in London would be thrown away.

On Boxing Day I called them after spending the day volunteering at a special temporary shelter for homeless people who were unserved in the time between Christmas and New Year, when the social services they depended on were shut for the festive period. My job was to help process people who came in because they had immigration problems: a group of young men from South America who'd been caught sleeping on the floor of the chicken restaurant that employed them. An eighteen-year-old girl who'd been ejected from the home she shared with her husband and his mother. On the phone with my parents I drank a glass of white wine from Marks and Spencer and ate a ready meal beyond the means of my usual budget.

I realized, I said to them, recounting the day, looking out the Velux window over the council estates that stretched before me, up through Tower Hamlets and into Hackney, that there are so many people that have it so much worse than me. I guess I shouldn't feel so sorry for myself. I have to stop feeling so bad.

Well, said my dad, in his comforting baritone, that's

true, Jean. But that doesn't mean that you're not allowed to feel. People's problems are people's problems.

For all of the times that I can't remember what he said in a particular moment, that's one that I know: precise, and true.

I never saw Mark again, or not on purpose, not other than across a street or at a music festival, but I did continue working at the literary agency for five more months. My boss wanted me to go but she didn't actually have grounds to fire me. My incompetence was insufficient, so I had to keep going to work every day until I found another job. I went to interview after interview where women who were my prospective new bosses looked at my CV and said things like: Oh, well, we couldn't hire you, she'd be so upset that we poached you! and I laughed a choking laugh that probably broadcast how much she disliked me. Reading my boss's emails in the morning, combing through to delete the messages from African princes, I found one from one of her friends. Sorry you have to find a new assistant, he wrote. Make sure the new one is pretty.

On my final day, when I resigned to take a low-paid internship answering to one of my friends, anything to escape the toxic atmosphere, the boss gave me a mid-priced handbag and a large bouquet of fresh flowers.

Good luck, she said to me. And then: Don't write about us!

I won't, I said. I produced a smile. The smile was fake, but I did feel a little bit happy, that this woman who seemed to dislike me so much might think my writing could be a threat.

I watched her depart and then handed the bouquet to the friend who sat next to me. I returned the handbag to the shop. After my leaving drinks, I got on the Central Line and sobbed so hard, with such extravagance, that strangers, Londoners, the people who are possibly least in the world inclined to acknowledge the emotions of others, offered me tissues, or at least unused Pret a Manger napkins that they dug from the bottoms of handbags.

Thanks, I said, to the people with the paper goods. Thank you.

And then I became a writer, because there was nothing else to do.

5

What did I do next? I did internships. I took weird editorial jobs. I did unpaid work experience at newspapers. I went for drinks with senior male editors who pretended that they were interested in my writing but really just hoped that I'd sleep with them. I contributed articles to a scrappy, ambitious magazine run by friends of a friend in an old factory in Dalston. After nights of editing we'd go out and eat big plates of cheap Turkish stew, drink Efes and talk about how we were going to do great things and get our revenge on all of the older people in the media who had so far failed to recognize that we were destined to do great things.

In time, I started eking a living from words: blog posts, tiny book reviews, B2B magazines. Copywriting for a Danish shipping company, articles about innovations in office furniture. Occasional features for publications that my friends down the pub had heard of. For six months I wrote the view-from-a-woman column for a men's magazine that they ran with a byline illustration of a woman who was, let's say, more conventionally hot than me.

(It looks like Gisele Bündchen with brown hair, my friend Ella said, when I showed her the first issue with my column. She paused for a moment. You don't look like Gisele Bündchen, she said, as if that needed to be clarified.)

I dreamed of a full-time job on a newspaper, clutched the crumbs of occasional assignments and covered shifts at desks for absent low-level editors. But while I waited for that full-time job to happen (it didn't), I did what I could to make a living. My work was never about affording to be picky. That's why my favourite job was as a freelance writer for a magazine about conference travel, which is to say: a magazine for people who organized conferences. The writing itself was boring, detailed rundowns of hotel facilities and team-building day trips for men and maybe a few women who were unlike any people who I came into contact with in my real life.

But the assignments meant that all of a sudden I got to go on glamorous international trips, flying business class and staying in five-star hotels, places where I'd come back to my room in the evening to find that the cleaner hadn't just made the bed but put my toiletries on the bathroom counter in a straight line and placed my inhaler at a right angle to my novel on the bedside table. My assignments paid a decent day rate, indeed an incredible one once I billed the publisher for expenses. At home I was living on the knife-edge of ruin, secretly withdrawing cash from my credit-card account and pushing the machine-fresh stacks of bills, hot in my hands, back into my checking account. Waiting for freelance payments from dawdling accounts payable departments meant that I had to make hard choices about how I'd feed myself. Oatmeal could be OK two times a day. Three times was my limit. But when I went on these press trips I ate like a queen: Yes, I said, I'll have another helping, a second pass at the buffet. A second deep-fried dinner roll. Of course, please, bring me the dessert menu.

I also took shower after shower, standing up. How unique, I would think, as I shampooed my hair and watched suds run down the full length of my body, what an unusual and pleasant sensation. This could really catch on!

By now the water pressure in the flat on Cephas Street was so bad that in the colder months there were many hours a day where we had no water at all, and through a series of letters citing violation of UN human rights conventions, my neighbours and I had gotten our landlord to reduce the monthly rent by nearly half. When I described this problem to my friends, that we couldn't wash ourselves or flush the toilet, my friends expressed regret but never suggested that we move. This was London, then, and maybe now: the inconvenience of being never quite clean and perpetually dehydrated was a small price to pay for an affordable home in a cool East London neighbourhood.

One day, I'd think, as I turned on the bathroom taps at full blast and watched no water at all come out of them, One day I'll write about this as evidence of all of the suffering I did for my art.

Like many of my writing jobs I got the conference travel one because a man sent me an email. I was unhappy that this was the route, that more often than not the men who emailed me to offer me employment cited some evidence that they knew that I was young and a woman. But when the emails came in and offered me things, it was hard to say no. Will you meet me for coffee? this particular man said in his email, and I said: No, because I didn't want to go on a date with a father-aged man, and then he wrote back and said: Would you like to write for my magazine about conference travel? It pays, and I wrote back and said, Sure! and he replied: Great, let's meet for coffee to discuss it.

The man who had sent me the email turned out to be about fifty, and when I entered the Costa near the Farringdon tube station he looked a bit alarmed by the way in which I was a real young human woman. He wore a wedding ring and spoke in a quiet voice. Afterwards he sent me on my first assignment, which was to Estonia, and I was very excited until someone said to me: What if he's there in the hotel waiting for you! and then I felt very stressed. My time working with older men in journalism had given me the sense that this was a real possibility: that career advancement was a tightrope between taking advantage of opportunity and being taken advantage of.

When I checked in the receptionist said, There's a gift for you in your room, and I rode the elevator with overwhelming fear and nausea, imagining the editor reclining on a crisp white duvet cover strewn with rose petals. But the gift was a paperweight, lucite with 'Tallinn!' painted across the base in gold.

There was no reason for me to visit the destinations I was going to, because all of the information I needed to write the boring articles was on the internet. But the editor of the magazine didn't seem to know that much about the internet, so I took the opportunity offered to trot around cities with people who worked in municipal conference bureaus – did you know that people work in municipal conference bureaus? I did not – and ask the questions I knew they wanted to hear.

How many chairs are in this room? I would say, as if that information was not on the internet. Someone would say how many chairs and then I would nod and pretend to write it down. Then I accepted the stacks of brochures that they handed me. I disposed of them in the trash of the ladies' room of whichever airport terminal I was departing from.

After my trip to Tallinn I got to go to Mauritius. Mauritius is an island in the middle of the Indian Ocean: that's what you have to tell people who haven't heard of Mauritius, which is maybe an OK place for some people to not have heard of. That's how small and remote it is: the closest place is Madagascar, but it's still hundreds of miles away from there. I'd heard of Mauritius before as a place to go on honeymoon, and indeed when I got to the gate at Heathrow for my flight to Mauritius – twelve hours, direct – I seemed to be the only person there who was not nervously twisting a fresh wedding ring around the fourth finger on my left hand. Among the nervous twisters I felt very young, even though I was twenty-seven and had already attended a number of my friends' weddings. But not since Paul had there been a man in my life in the presence of whom I could say the phrase 'my boyfriend' with confidence.

In the queue to get on to the plane one of the ring-twisters said to his new wife: You've had more last names than you've had hot dinners! and I thought to myself: I wish I was loved.

In Mauritius there was a pineapple cut in a fancy shape in my bedroom and towels rolled into swans and also a typhoon. The typhoon was some of the worst weather in Mauritius in decades, so bad that they'd closed all of the schools in the country. The hotel I was staying in was not designed to be a place where you spent time indoors other than sleeping, and so each morning I walked from my room to the open porch where you ate breakfast and arrived at the breakfast porch sodden, despite my umbrella.

Maybe, I thought, I should feel pity for the people who are here on their once-in-a-lifetime honeymoon and having it ruined by this weather. But when I got to the breakfast porch and no one was eating breakfast besides me and a solitary man with the top part of his wetsuit rolled down and tied around his waist, I thought: But the people on honeymoon are all having sex, whereas I can only eat this delicious Mauritian breakfast custard and wonder if I should talk to this man in a wetsuit.

I ate another breakfast custard.

I was in Mauritius for six days and towards the very end of the trip the weather cleared up. I had some time free after viewing many conference rooms, so I went to the private beach that was owned by the hotel. It had white sand and perfect aquamarine water and palm trees and it was exactly the kind of place you would want to come with the person you loved so much you'd just pledged to spend the rest of your life with them. Or yourself.

On the beach there was a system of flags to indicate

your desire for service: if you wanted someone to come over and offer you a selection of delicious treats from the hotel restaurant you stabbed your blue flag in the sand next to you. If you did not want to be disturbed by someone offering you a selection of delicious treats from the hotel restaurant you had a red flag to stab into the sand next to you, lest anyone should bother you with offers of pleasure.

The red flag felt like a degree of imperiousness unlike any I had ever encountered. What would it be like, I wondered, to be so rich and important that you feel like you have to tell people not to serve you?

But I used my blue flag to get a nice man to bring me a club sandwich, and a cool glass of beet juice that sparkled its deep pink-purple hue in the sun.

How can I make my life one in which this is a normal occurrence? I wondered, as I drank the juice, and for just that moment, such a life felt possible.

I had never been so far from home.

The next morning I went to the toilet and when I got up I saw that the contents were bright red, and my legs buckled. I have colon cancer! I thought, the disease that my grandmother died of so young, the thing that my father had warned me about so often. I hadn't been eating much fibre on my trip to Mauritius, and now here I was, dying on my own on an island in the middle of the Indian Ocean. Who would come and help me? I had literally never been so far from home, and now I was not just far from home but alone in a leading international honeymoon destination, dying of colon cancer.

Then I remembered how much beet juice I'd had to drink on the beach the day before.

How silly! I thought. How paranoid am I to think that I am doomed to get colon cancer just because my father is so preoccupied with it!

How wonderful to be young and alone and free in Mauritius, in a body I knew so little about.

6

Sometimes when I tell people about what my life in London was like, they think I was having a bad time. The no-water flat, the bad jobs, the men who failed to appreciate me. The constant damp, the mould, the pallid greasy food.

In fact, I loved living in London.

I loved the flat at the top of the church. I loved its quirks, its slanted ceilings that I often hit my head on. I loved the classy laminate floors that almost looked nice when I vacuumed them, which was a thing I did once in a while.

I loved having people over for dinner. I loved the Thanksgiving when I invited pretty much everyone I knew on the specific day, a Thursday night, and roasted a turkey in the oven and made a pumpkin cheesecake and wore an orange dress. I loved how there weren't enough places to sit down, not really, I loved how I had to plunder Adam's apartment downstairs for all his chairs and also for his oven, in which I roasted potatoes to a near-inedible blackness. I loved when I went downstairs to fetch the potatoes and Adam's father happened to be visiting and he looked on in bemusement while this American woman in an orange dress slammed through the front door without knocking, said an abrupt hello, and slammed out again with a tray of potatoes.

I loved living upstairs from Adam. It was just a coincidence that Adam moved in downstairs, Adam who had been in Paris all of those years ago, right there in that bar with Lisa and me and Paul, as Paul and I fell in love. Adam lived directly beneath us and when one morning he texted me that he had been offered a job as a lawyer I already knew because he had been blasting MIA's 'Paper Planes' at full volume on a loop. It was early on a Saturday morning and I was hungover as I always was on Saturday mornings, and when I went downstairs to tell Adam to please turn the music off, Adam cried out, JEANO, I'M NAKED, and I said, I KNOW, YOU ARE PLAYING THIS SONG AT A VOLUME THAT COULD ONLY BE ACCOMPANIED BY NAKED DANCING.

I loved that on dark cold evenings when I rode my bike into the courtyard in front of the church I'd ring the bike bell. The bell made an adorable tinging noise that was not appropriate for admonishing men in cars who were trying to take my life, but was perfect for alerting a neighbour to one's arrival home. Adam would lean his head out the window and shout, JEANO, WANT A CUP OF TEA? and I would say YES even though I don't really like tea. Adam made tea in a pot, not in a mug, and the pot wore a knitted cosy. Keep it cosy, Jeano, Adam would say when I made the tea and didn't put the cosy on, and I would say, I'm AMERICAN, OK? and Adam would shake his head in disgust.

I loved that Adam knew my ex-boyfriend and I knew his

ex-girlfriend and because of this we did not see each other as romantic prospects, not at all, not even when my friends thought I should, not even when my friends said it as if it was an original idea: You should marry Adam! and I said, No, never, with uncharacteristic certainty.

I loved that Adam and I knew each other best at a time in our lives when we needed to get to know ourselves more than we needed to be in love with other people. I loved that in the period of time that our friendship was most intense we both had a variety of superficial romances that went nowhere because for that period of time, in that year, we probably did not need them. We did not need to invest that much in the future – not in terms of focus, or of worry.

In London I loved going to parties. I loved the time of our lives when every weekend night was a party. I loved that we went to the kinds of parties in East London that were so cool it took my breath away with amazement, that I'd achieved such a thing, loose associations with people who threw parties in warehouses where people did pole dances that were performance art and everyone was high on cocaine and MDMA. I loved that I got into these parties and I even loved that I kind of hated these parties, that once inside I never felt comfortable. I loved that I would then get on my heavy Dutch bicycle and ride home, at two or three or four in the morning, through the dark and empty streets of Dalston and Bethnal Green.

I loved that I felt safe doing this, even when I couldn't get into the locked courtyard around the church and had to climb on top of a skip to jump over the fence in my green silky Primark shift dress. I loved that I dressed like an eccentric English person who anticipated a tea party around every corner, hence the reason that I was wearing a green silky Primark shift dress on that particular occasion.

I loved eating bagels on Brick Lane and debating which of the two near-identical bagel shops was the superior bagel shop, which was a question that could be debated for hours every hungover Sunday and never resolved.

I loved the rare times I saw my byline in print in the broadsheets. I loved reading newspaper articles that I'd written on the tube, spreading the paper in an inconvenient way, to see if anyone noticed. I loved feeling like I occasionally got away with being important because I was an outsider, and because I was an outsider people could not make decisions about the kind of person I was in the way that people in England seemed to like to decide about other English people.

I loved being young, although of course at the time I didn't know that being young was what I was, or what I loved. Except for one time when a bendy bus nearly crushed me on my bike as I rode it up Oxford Street, I did not spend my time contemplating how and when I was likely to die.

For nine years I loved living in London. And then I didn't love it any more.

7

Three things happened in the year that I turned thirty that made me know it was time for me to leave London.

The first thing: I broke up with Frank.

Frank and I had been together for a year when things started to unravel between us. The reason that they began to unravel was that we had been together a year. It was August when we reached the anniversary, a thing that seemed like it should be a milestone. In the time we spent together – one or two evenings a week, twenty-four hours over the course of a weekend – we talked about whether we should do something to celebrate. A weekend away. A fancy dinner. We talked and talked about how we should mark our time together, but we never got past the talking. Instead, we went to a wedding, the marriage of one of Frank's friends from high school.

When Frank and I had gotten together the previous August, in 2010, it was because we were perfect for each other. That's to say we were both at a point in our lives where we felt like we should be in a relationship. I was nearing thirty, Frank a year or two older.

We'd both spent years knocking around London with gangs of friends, but the gangs were thinning. The gangs were getting married, having children, leaving the city to go and live with the people they'd married and the children they'd had. Our friends were building lives around people they loved more than they loved us. This was only right, but it did not always feel good. I didn't want to be the last person standing, and maybe Frank didn't either, so when we met and there was a bit of an attraction, maybe that's why it happened: we became a couple. After all the years spending time with men who didn't love me, when Frank, a very nice person, showed interest in being my boyfriend, it seemed like the right thing to do. Frank didn't love me either, not in the way that I needed, but unlike the other men, he was willing to stick around.

The thing that Frank and I seemed to have most in common was our mutual desire not to have too much feeling. As I watched my friends get swept up in grand romances and clapped while they walked down grand aisles at their grand weddings, I began to suspect that there was a problem with my expectations. Why should I be so lucky to meet the love of my life? I had tried that before. Maybe I'd tried that enough. If I wanted to be in a relationship, I thought, why shouldn't I do it with someone who's simply very nice? That's what I was thinking when I met Frank.

I shouldn't have been with Frank for a year: I should have broken up with him the previous Christmas. For Christmas I knitted Frank a tie, because knitted ties were Frank's signature look, so much so that my friends called him 'Knitted Tie'. Is Knitted Tie coming out tonight? they'd ask, and I'd usually say: No, because a thing about Frank and I that didn't work very well was that I loved to spend time with other people and he did not. Sometimes, if I objected enough, if I wheedled and pouted, Frank would join some kind of group activity – that is, after all, how my friends knew that he wore knitted ties, because they had seen them knotted around his neck. But more often than I would have liked to, I would show up to places alone. And maybe part of the reason that my friends called him Knitted Tie was because they didn't know him well enough to remember his name.

I knitted Frank a tie because knitting was something that I was good at and because I thought that handmade gifts were thoughtful, and also because I knew already that he loved knitted ties. It was early enough in our relationship that I still thought maybe Frank could grow to love me, and I could grow to love Frank. But Frank regarded my handiwork – it was purple, because that was my favourite colour, and he didn't have a purple knitted tie already – and Frank said: Well, thanks. Later on, when I asked him why he hadn't worn the tie that I'd knitted him, Frank said: It doesn't fit.

It's a tie, I said, of course it fits! but Frank said, It doesn't. A couple of weeks later, in a restaurant with some of my friends – Frank had come to dinner, which was somewhat out of character, and maybe because he felt bad about the tie – Adam's sister, who was a teacher and thus very good at expressing herself, said: Why aren't you wearing the tie? and Frank said, again, It doesn't fit! and she pointed at him, practically prodding his chest, and said, YOU WILL WEAR THE TIE, AT LEAST ONCE YOU WILL WEAR IT.

And still he never wore the tie.

I should have taken this as a sign that Frank wasn't the man for me, that I should only love a man who would wear anything that I knitted for him. But still I thought maybe it was better to be with Frank than to be alone.

Although he did not love me, Frank was pretty kind to me, and I hope I was pretty kind to him. We enjoyed each other's company, and when we were parted for longer than usual, we were happy to see each other again. But not hungry. We talked about books and art and work and friends. But we didn't really talk about feelings.

In that August, at the wedding of his friends from high school, Frank and I were on the invite B-list: when we arrived, along with the other high-school friends, the ceremony and the wedding meal had already passed, the hem of the wedding gown stained green from wet grass, the eyes of the A-list guests – close family, closer friends – were a little misty, from alcohol and gravy and emotion. Some people seemed tired.

On the way to the venue, Frank and I had a small argument. We were ratty. It started on the train and then it escalated when we arrived. Something to do with taking a wrong turn from the station. We picked our way down a damp and thorny path, and then back again. I was wearing a blue summer dress and silver shoes, with stacked wooden heels. My legs were bare and the thorns scratched them. Frank was wearing a suit and a tie that I didn't knit him. I sighed heavily at Frank, and Frank sighed heavily at me, but by the time we got to the wedding, we were friends again. Though maybe not much more than friends.

I asked Frank's high-school friends to tell me about what Frank was like in high school, because that's a thing that you ask high-school friends about your boyfriend. The high-school friends were friendly, and the wives and girlfriends of the high-school friends were kind and welcoming, as if I was now one of them. They suggested that Frank and I come to their homes for dinners or that we all go out for drinks, and I smiled and said that would be nice, though I did not think we ever would.

But I looked at my boyfriend, surrounded by people who had known and loved him for most of his life, and I thought about how he was pleasant and handsome and a good man. In a way, I thought, he is exceptional. When it started to rain we took our drinks from the outdoor bar and continued the conversations in a corridor of the stately home that was hosting the wedding, packed elbow-to-elbow like seatless passengers on a hot and overcrowded train.

Frank and I had spent a lot of time together on trains that year. By then I was working as a travel editor, and we went to stay in fancy hotels together: me, the professional; him, the plus one. We took trains to the countryside, to the Continent. And sometimes, somewhere in a posh hotel or an art gallery, or drinking coffee in a dirty Parisian tabac, I felt I adored him. I'd scrutinize him as he scrutinized a map or a menu and I'd think yes, maybe I could love you. And then we'd go home, and sometimes on the way we'd talk about whether we should move in together as if that was something we wanted to do, but we didn't make any plans.

Eventually it was time for dancing. There was a live band, led by an aged Mancunian, with Rod Stewart hair. For some reason he was wearing army fatigues suitable for doing battle in a desert. The music was Northern Soul. The floor was packed with satin dresses and hair gel and beer-odoured breath. I want to have a soul-singing Rod Stewart lookalike from Manchester in desert army fatigues at my wedding, I shouted in Frank's ear, and I grinned at him, and he grinned back at me, but I felt sad, and I think he felt sad, because I knew, and I think he knew, that we loved each other in the particular way that two people who were brought together by their mutual fear of love do. With restraint. Within reason. With no risk of the kind of love that might one day culminate in a wedding disco with a soul-singing aged Rod Stewart lookalike.

The band played 'Mustang Sally'. I took Frank's hand in mine and we danced some more. We stuck it out until November, because I think we both hoped that what we had was enough: that we could avoid the fear we shared of wanting more.

When he ended it, over the phone, it was because I had invited him to go to America with me, for Thanksgiving: I realized, he said, that I'd rather not go, that I'd rather stay in London and work on my art projects.

I cried and swore, but I was mostly angry with myself, for not getting there first. Three days later I felt OK about Frank. Free, in fact. So free that I began to wonder what, exactly, was the reason that I still lived in London.

That was the first thing that made me think: Maybe it's time to go.

The second thing.

The second thing happened at work, not long after Frank and I broke up, after I started to feel very free. A month or so later.

I was working at an ad agency by then: I'd become a copywriter. And the thing happened at the office Christmas party.

When he heard what happened, my friend Rich remarked, If he was planning to grope some breasts, he should have known better than to grope yours.

This was true.

I'd worked in the ad agency for only five months, but had already established my reputation as a humourless feminist. Just a few weeks in, when I was the only woman in a team working on a project an art director made a rape joke to the room.

Hey, I said to the art director, do you know what jokes are never funny?

When someone played a song about sexual assault on the office loudspeaker one morning before lunch, I wrote an all-company email suggesting it be taken off the rotation.

Hey, I wrote. Can we not listen to songs about rape in the office?

I remained stony-faced in meetings while a member of the senior management team described new female hires with respect to their hotness, their blondeness, called out to the men who the company director reckoned would want to have a go at fucking them.

Is it normal, I said to my friend who also worked at a London ad agency, for a company director to describe how fuckable new women employees are? Do they do that at your company?

No, said my friend.

What I did not do was take the warning seriously. On my first day, the woman introducing me to the company walked me around the large open-plan office and told me everyone's name. I shook their hands. Watch out for him, an account manager said, in a jolly voice, while I shook the hand of the man who would later assault me, he's a sleaze-bag.

I laughed. I was a grown-up woman. I was thirty years old. I had some seniority. I was not worried. I was not scared of him.

I was not a seventeen-year-old girl being fondled from behind by another bit-part actor in the school play each time we stood behind the backstage curtains, waiting for our cue.

(You must be imagining it, said a friend, when finally I was brave enough to tell someone, to ask for help. Why would he touch you? my friend said. He has a really hot girlfriend.

I told no one else.)

I was not a twenty-three-year-old waitress whose manager was rubbing his hands down the front of her apron, below her waist.

(I waited until his shift was done, I immediately resigned to the deputy manager, I refused to make a formal complaint because it was just a waitressing job, because I couldn't bear the idea of being made to see him again, or the idea of not being believed.)

I was not a twenty-six-year-old on work experience at a national newspaper, fetching coffee and opening post and being slapped on the thigh by the editor with a sex toy that he had lying around on his desk.

(Everyone saw it, everyone laughed, I did nothing because there was nothing official about work experience, it was not covered under the company HR policy, and because it seemed likely that if I complained I'd never work at the newspaper again.)

Of course it was an office Christmas party groping: and that's what some people said to me immediately after it happened, when I pushed the man off me and fled to the other side of the room: It's the office Christmas party. As if taking a colleague's breasts, one in each hand, and twisting her nipples through her dress and bra is an appropriate way to celebrate the festive season. I'm American, I said, with the confidence of a woman living under the governance of Barack Obama. I'm American, and this is unacceptable. I left the party and I got in a cab and I called one of my friends and I told her what happened and I cried.

But I also knew that it was going to be OK: I was a grown woman. I was in a senior position. This time, no one would not believe me, and no one would laugh.

I made a complaint. I wrote the man an email, dripping with sarcasm. Non-consensual sexual contact with your female colleagues is not an appropriate way to celebrate the festive season, I wrote. I made an accompanying PowerPoint presentation, to illustrate my point. It was the second time in my life that I had made a PowerPoint presentation. The PowerPoint presentation had a Venn diagram, two circles. In one circle, I typed 'appropriate behaviour towards female colleagues'. In the other circle, I typed 'sexual touching'. I animated an arrow. It slid between the circles on a click. Underneath, I wrote 'no intersection'.

I added an exclamation mark, for emphasis.

I sent the email to the man and I cc'd his manager. I have attached a short PowerPoint presentation, I wrote in my email to him, which may help to clear up any questions you have about appropriate ways to celebrate the festive season.

The manager came over immediately and apologized, as if it was his fault. I'm so sorry, the manager said. Thank you, I said. I'm going to escalate it to HR, the manager said.

Thank you, I said, I don't want him to lose his job.

Of course this was not true, but it is what I said.

(What I actually meant, I think, was that I didn't want it to be my fault that he lost his job. I was a grown woman, I was in a senior position, no one would or could think that I was making it up. But I still felt at fault. I had attended the office Christmas party. I had drunk a cocktail. I had worn a dress with a neckline that dipped below my collarbone. I had engaged in a friendly enough relationship with a known sleazebag because the office manager had assigned me to sit at a desk next to his every day.)

He slunk into the office late, the morning after. I looked at him. I'm sorry, he said, I have no memory of what happened last night. I looked at him some more. Huh, I said.

Later in the day, he packed up to go home. It was the last day of work before the Christmas break. Merry Christmas, I said to him, even though I didn't mean it.

We're dealing with it, the company director said when I returned after the holiday break. I'm so sorry.

Thank you, I said.

A few days later, I was called to a meeting with the HR director.

There's not enough evidence to fire him, the HR director said to me. I stared at the HR director. I blinked.

There are not enough witnesses, she continued.

I am a witness, I said.

We've given him a serious punishment, said the HR director. He's on permanent probation, a final warning. I can't tell you all the conditions of his probation for confidentiality reasons, but I can tell you he's no longer allowed to drink at office functions. One drink and he's out.

He's still allowed to attend office functions? I said. You do realize this means I will never again attend an office function.

Oh, said the HR director.

I can't work with him, I said.

We were told that you would be OK with working with him, said the HR director.

Who told you that? I said. That's not true.

Oh, said the HR director, again.

I left the building.

I will not come back, I said in an email, to HR and the company partners, until you have offered me a satisfactory solution to this problem.

The company director called me. Please meet me, the company director said. I won't come to the office, I said. We met in a coffee shop. The company director looked fraught. He offered me a coffee. I refused. The company director drank one. He added a lot of sugar.

The thing is, the company director said, in a slow voice, this is an issue of consent versus non-consent.

There is no way I would consent to this, I said. There is no one who could do this to me. If it was a stranger, I would have gotten the police. If it was a friend, I would have terminated our friendship. If it was an intimate partner, I would have ended the relationship.

I said all this as if my view on the boundaries of sexual contact were a reasonable thing to discuss with the company director of a place where I worked.

Well, he said, Jean, I just don't know what to do.

You'll have to figure something out, I said.

I left and worked from home.

I really just want to go to work, I said to my friends.

Of course, they said.

It could have been worse, I said to my friends.

My friends looked at me. I looked at them. There was nothing more to say after that.

I waited for some days but I heard nothing from the company. So I wrote a long list of demands, conditions in which I would return to work. I would not ever have to work with him on a project again. I would not be in a room with him with the door closed. He would not be allowed to approach or speak to me in the office. He would have his desk moved so that it was far away from mine.

The company agreed to the conditions. I went back to work.

But I still had to see the man every day. And every time that I saw him I remembered the look in his beady, glassy eyes, and the feeling of his hands on me, gripping and twisting.

He was working on the company's most interesting project. Because I refused to work with him, they hired a freelancer to do what would have been my job. I sat at my desk and applied for other jobs at other companies.

I avoided eye contact. I pretended I didn't notice the people who didn't talk to me any more. And the people who knew all the details but who didn't say anything. I felt alone. To them, I wanted to say, What if this happened to a woman you loved? But I didn't, because the difference between a woman who can be sexually assaulted and a woman who can't is not whether a man loves her.

A colleague left the company. She had leaving drinks on a Friday night. I had a cold, so I didn't go. On Saturday morning another colleague called me. Guess who was drinking at the party last night, she said. I was speechless. I'm not even sure it's an official company function, I said, I don't think they'll care.

I hung up the phone and sat down on the floor of my bedroom and cried.

I was wrong. On Tuesday they fired him. I was in a meeting for two hours and when I came back to my desk

I had a stack of emails. At the top was one from one of the colleagues who hadn't spoken to me since it happened. Just so you know, the colleague wrote, he's my friend, but I support you.

Why do you support me? I thought.

I looked at the other emails. Furthest down in my inbox was one from the company director, sent to the whole company, announcing that he had been fired. More recent, an email from the company director, asking if we could speak for a moment.

Sure, I said.

We went into the boardroom.

Today, said the company director, is the worst day of my life at this company.

I'm sorry, I said, even though I was not sorry.

I went for a walk around the block. Should I feel bad about this, I thought to myself, that he has been fired because I do not believe that it is acceptable to sexually assault one's colleagues at the office Christmas party?

I decided I should not feel bad about it.

That was the second thing.

The third thing.

The third thing that happened was the Queen's Diamond Jubilee Flotilla.

I really liked the word 'flotilla'. I'm sure I'd heard it before, in other contexts, but now I loved 'flotilla'. I was charmed by the idea that the nation was going to celebrate one woman holding one unelected position of leadership for sixty years by sending some stately boats down a river.

I was amazed that the river would be thronged on either side by people, twenty-first-century people, observing the stately boats. I liked the way 'flotilla' felt in my mouth as I pronounced it, slow and drawn out. I talked about it as much as I could. Are you excited about the flo-till-a? I said to the people at work who were still speaking to me. Sure? some of them said. I can't wait for the flo-till-a! I exclaimed in response.

The flotilla was on a Sunday in early June. People around the country who weren't available to stand by the side of the Thames and watch the stately boats float past had been encouraged to hold old-fashioned street parties, to hang bunting from trees, to serve sponge cakes and tea from sets of china awarded to female ancestors in honour of achieving husbands.

I didn't care for the royal family as an institution, not once I realized that the chances of me becoming a princess were nil. When Prince William married Catherine Middleton the previous year, granting the whole nation a long weekend, Frank and I had fled on a first-thing-in-the-morning Eurostar to Paris, to make a point about our Republican position. When we arrived, we were very tired, and it was too early to check in to our hotel room, so we went around the corner and sat in a tabac, arriving just in time to see Prince William marry Catherine Middleton on the screens of the tabac's dusty televisions. We sipped cafés noirs and ate hard croissants and felt resentment.

But I didn't think I would resent the flotilla: it was an antiquated event designed to celebrate an antiquated woman's many decades holding an antiquated office in a country that was, it could not be denied, sometimes very antiquated.

The sky was a classic English grey that morning, but Rich and his partner Laura had planned a party at their home, in any case: instead of jostling elbows with other fans of stately boats on the riverside, we'd enjoy the comfort of their flat while watching the procession on the television. When I climbed on my bike to cycle the five miles there it was just beginning to rain, but by the time I arrived it was sheeting down and I could no longer see where I was going through my glasses. Rich opened the door and regarded me and retreated. He returned with a towel.

You'll want to dry off before you come in, he said, as much for the sake of the apartment as for the sake of my sodden body.

Enthusiasm is flagging, Rich continued, as I dried off. You need to do what you can to improve the enthusiasm.

Inside the living room, there was indeed little enthusiasm. There were sandwiches and Victoria sponge and several of the cheeriest people I knew, but there was also a devastating spectacle, the pride of a nation represented by a joyless and troubling procession of boats listing to and fro in the storm. I was transfixed: the sheets of rain were coating the television cameras just as they had my glasses, making it difficult to see. The boats drifted down the river, manned by soaked skippers. On a special barge, the Royal Family observed with gritted teeth.

The Duchess of Cambridge is wearing Alexander

McQueen! a commentator trilled, while Kate Middleton wiped visible mucus from her nose with the edge of her sleeve.

What a terrific, terrific celebration! another commentator declared, cutting to a group of weeping, sodden school children.

We're going to have an RAF flyover! cried a further presenter. He paused. Oh, he said, actually, it's been paused due to the weather.

This is a total shitshow! I said. This would never happen in America!

Our spirits aren't dampened! said the presenter, much like my mother on a long-ago Scottish beach caravan holiday, when she had to pretend each morning that we were having a good time even though we were kept awake all night by the howling of wind that seemed to threaten to pick the caravan up and dump it in the sea. We're having a wonderful holiday! my brave mother said in those mornings, as we squeezed around the alcove table in the caravan kitchen, sniffling from summer colds as we slurped Weetabix and ate toasted Hovis spread with margarine.

The BBC presenters held the mood of the nation in their hands. If they were honest, if they were true, if they said: This flotilla is unbelievably shit! Kate Middleton just wiped her nose on her sleeve! then Britain would fall apart.

I realized then that I could never truly embrace the national resignation. I could never belong.

Later that evening, I called my parents. They'd watched a bit of the flotilla on the American news.

How are you? said my mother.

I'm despondent about the flotilla, I said.

Oh, said my dad, it wasn't so bad. I liked watching the boats on the Thames.

I think I might need to leave England, I said.

We all laughed.

That's an extreme reaction, my mother said.

I think I hate it here, I said.

That was the third thing. In late September that year, I left London for Berlin.

8

How happy was I in Berlin? I was very happy. Or I believe I was, although when I reflect I do wonder whether my happiness seemed more acute because my time in Berlin came just before I moved to Brooklyn, like when you make a beam of light in a drawing by smudging thick lines of charcoal in the area surrounding it.

If things had been different, people sometimes ask me, Would you have liked to stay in Berlin? and I say, I don't know. I imagine that I would have, but that's really just imagining. Because that is not what happened. Things were not different.

In Berlin I lived on Helmholtzplatz. It was a square – a rectangle, really – named after a physicist, destroyed in the war, later a place where East German resisters would sometimes meet and make whispered plans, because unlike their apartments the Stasi had not wired it with bugs. But in 2012 Helmholtzplatz was just a park, with a play area for children, some gentle hills with itchy grass. Weatherproof concrete ping-pong tables that people played ping-pong on when the weather was nice, and which alcoholics used as surfaces for large beers and long naps when the weather was not.

My apartment on Helmholtzplatz was in the back of a

pre-war apartment building, through a courtyard, and it didn't have a balcony, which people familiar with such matters informed me made it not such a good Berlin apartment. But I loved that apartment with my whole heart. It had whitewashed walls and wooden floorboards and high ceilings, and once I got the furniture that I needed to fill it, it was still rather empty.

Once, early in my time there, a friend from university came to visit, she was passing through Berlin on her way to or from a conference, and she said: When are you going to get more furniture, Jean? and I said, What more furniture do I need? and she said, Yes, I see what you mean. This was the first time in my life that I owned any furniture at all. In London, for the most part, I'd lived in flats that rented complete with other people's sagging mattresses and sofas. For the last year and a half of my time there I'd sublet the home of a woman who charged me a lower-than-low price for her beautiful little one-bed flat in Islington, but removed only a few of her possessions, so that I went to sleep each night under a giant print of a photo of Audrey Hepburn on one wall, and an equally giant print of Marilyn Monroe on the other. Now my *Wohnung* in Berlin was several rooms that were really my own, with my own pictures on the walls, and a coat rack I'd hung myself by the front door and which came crashing to the ground every time someone came over and hung their coat on it. Sorry! the person who was visiting would say, and I'd say, Don't worry about it, and then I'd hang the coat rack up again and think: This place is really mine.

The kitchen in my apartment on Helmholtzplatz was very small, a cupboard with a window, really, and in the morning I would make my breakfast – an egg fried in butter, dark rye toast with jam that I fried in a pan because I didn't have a toaster. I drank black coffee that I made in a stovetop espresso pot that the last tenant had left behind, the kind that heats until the coffee erupts up into the pot like a surprise. I often overboiled it. While I ate my breakfast I'd watch the sun come up, and if it was still dark I'd watch the couple in the kitchen across the courtyard, two men making their own breakfasts: they drank smoothies, they often wore matching red tracksuits. The men across the courtyard were close enough that I would have noticed if they changed their morning routine, but far enough that if I met them on the street wearing anything but the tracksuits, I would not recognize them. In Berlin, my relationship with the couple in the tracksuits felt like exactly the amount of intimacy that I wanted to start my days.

Sometimes I wondered if I would ever have a man in my kitchen in Berlin, someone for whom I would cook a second egg and a second piece of dark rye toast, but the truth is that when I was living in my apartment on Helmholtzplatz I was not really trying to meet any men, and that was part of what was making me happy. In Berlin, couples sleep in double beds but with their own separate single duvets, rather than sharing one, and when I went to IKEA with my friend Claudia I said: Claudia, should I buy another duvet, just in case? and Claudia said: You can wait until you need it. I never did. But most nights I felt perfectly cosy.

Over nine years in London, quite a lot of men had hurt my feelings. The city was full of street corners that reminded me of bad partings, park benches where men had made me cry, restaurants where I'd gazed in candlelight at faces I now hoped I'd never see again. In Berlin, I had space. Or the space had nothing on me. *Noch nicht.*

When I got a job offer in the summer of 2012 and the job was in Berlin I did not hesitate. My discontent with London had reached an all-time high post-flotilla. Earlier in the summer, my five-years-younger sister had married her boyfriend in Edinburgh. How do you feel about that, your younger sister getting married? people asked me when they heard the news, and I said: Fine! I would not want to marry her boyfriend! which everyone agreed was a good thing for me to not want to do.

When Elspeth sent me a wedding invitation, it was addressed to Jean Hannah Edelstein And Guest, and she followed up by saying: You can invite anyone you like to come with you! And I said, I could have two And Guests if I feel like it, because our parents are paying for it! Which was maybe not a thing that a five-years-older sister who was totally fine with her younger sister getting married would say.

I went without a date. And when our father gave a charming speech at their wedding, describing how my sister used to ride her small bike for hours in counterclockwise circles in the driveway, I wept: not so much because I was moved by his words, but because it was a few months after his lung-cancer diagnosis. His skin was broken out, a side effect of his chemotherapy, and I knew that he would not live long enough to give that kind of speech for me.

When I applied for the job in Berlin, I thought: I probably won't move to Berlin, but when I got the job I thought: I don't have any reason not to move to Berlin.

Some of my friends were dubious about my choice.

Why Berlin? they said.

Berlin is a place I have always wanted to live, ever since the first time I visited, I said, But I never thought I'd get a job there, because I don't really speak German. This will be the best of both worlds: a great job where I can speak English, and also an opportunity for the kind of immersion that I need to finally learn to speak German properly!

Do you really want to learn to speak German? said my friends.

Of course I do! I said. I studied German in school for five years! I will become fluent and it will be really useful, as long as I continue living in Germany! And then the moment I leave it will become useless.

OK, they said.

In German, 'Edelstein' is an old-fashioned word for a jewel, a diamond. In direct translation: noble stone. My German friends told me that it's terribly cute, but it's also like wearing a sign that says: I'm Jewish.

When my brother visited Germany as a teenager, on a school exchange, he told me that he noticed a curious phenomenon. I thought it was a German thing to introduce yourself by stating your age, he said, to say, Ich bin Jürgen und ich bin eins-und-dreizig Jahre alt, but then when one of them insisted on shaking my hand because I was Jewish, I realized that they wanted me to know that they weren't old enough to have been in the war.

Did you explain? I said. Did you tell him that you weren't actually Jewish?

Yes, said my brother, I told him that my mother wasn't Jewish, but he just looked at me and said, No, you are a Jew.

One of my friends in London was married to a German man. On a night out before I left London, he leaned in close and cooed in my ear.

You know, he said, so many Germans are going to want to have sex with you because your name is Edelstein!

OK, I said.

My interest was piqued.

In German, I was very extreme, because I had a limited vocabulary and a strong personality. At the office we were given free German classes: it was a perk, along with unlimited bars of Ritter Sport chocolate, many days of vacation, a thousand euros to spend a year on going to the gym or learning to throw ceramic pots, to make us feel like we had a life beyond the blue-lit glow of our laptops. I was in one of the most advanced classes in the Berlin office because of my five years of school German, which was more than most non-Germans in the company had.

Was ist Kunst? a page in my German textbook asked me, What is art? and I looked at the eight photographs, of paintings and street art and a pile of trash, and I announced to the room: Alles ist Kunst, Everything is art, because that way I wouldn't have to say anything else.

Wirklich? said my teacher, Really? Alles ist Kunst? and I nodded, as if my brevity was born from intellect rather than ignorance. Assembling a sentence of any further length was impossible: I understand a lot of German, but when it comes to speaking, my vocabulary is *klein*. My classmate laughed: she got me.

Our teacher, who was earnest, did not. She frowned. *Sehr extreme*, the teacher said, Very extreme. *Genau*, I said, Indeed, with the shrug of a confident extremist, because one of the first things I learned when I moved to Berlin was that you can say Genau in response to most statements. Genau imparts an air of certainty that can bring a dignified end to a conversation whether or not you're sure what it is that you're Genau-ing about.

This is how you got an apartment in Berlin: you found a place on the internet and then you went along at a designated hour when you looked at the apartment alongside maybe a dozen or perhaps fifty other people who were looking at the apartment. You thought about whether you could envision the apartment without the fifty other people in it, and in that envisioning, whether the apartment seemed nice. Then you filled out a long application form and hoped that the person deciding who will get to live in the apartment liked your form the best, maybe because of your wonderful handwriting or, as Claudia told me, if you wrote a cover letter full of moving personal details.

I went to see an apartment in Helmholtzplatz on a

Tuesday afternoon soon after I arrived in Berlin, and it seemed pretty perfect.

Entschuldigung, I said to the broker, in halting German, Excuse me, this apartment want I.

Fill out the form, the broker said.

OK, I said, friend mine help me out fill form. I don't good German speak.

Well, said the broker, he is already filling out the form so he is going to get the apartment.

He gestured at a man who was filling out the form with the confident flourish of someone who understands the dative case.

OK, I said, I will my friend take have the form away to help.

Genau, said the broker. Well, you can write down your name and phone number on this piece of paper and maybe I'll call you.

I wrote down my name and phone number.

Tschüss! I said to no one really at all. But then, as I walked down the corridor, I heard footsteps behind me. The broker.

EDELSTEIN! he said. That is a wonderful name.

Thank you, I said.

So beautiful, the broker said, beaming at me through the front door of the apartment. Such a special name!

Danke, I said again.

It's not British, said the broker. It's really, really German.

Genau, I said.

It's so special! said the broker. Where is your family from? WHERE IS YOUR FAMILY FROM?

WHAT DID YOUR FAMILY DO IN THE WAR?
I wanted to say, but instead I said: America. My family is American.

Edelstein! he said again. So special!

I smiled an uncomfortable smile as I clattered down the stairs.

I went home. Claudia helped me fill out the form and we submitted it to the broker with a letter full of moving personal details about my journey to Berlin, written by Claudia in its entirety.

The next day, she called the broker to find out about the apartment.

Jeani, she said, later on, I called the broker and it was extraordinary! He said that you can't have the apartment, it is already gone, but then he said, 'I have a special apartment for the special Edelstein.' So if you want it, you can have the apartment below the one you saw. He won't even put it on the market.

Genau, I said.

I was not lonely living on Helmholtzplatz. Claudia lived just around the corner, with her boyfriend Mirko. I called it The Platz, and they thought this was very funny, because it was bad Gerglish, but soon they called it that, too, at least when they were hanging out with me. Claudia and Mirko were why I had chosen to live on The Platz, so that Claudia and I could do things like drink coffee in the cafe on the ground floor of my building in the morning before we rode our bikes to work, or meet after work to drink Riesling in the charming bar on the Platz's south-east corner, which was called Liebling, which means 'darling', and which was exactly that.

I was not lonely, but unlike in London, where my evenings and weekends were stacked with social engagements, in Berlin I was often alone. I did not have the internet in my apartment in Berlin. This was because I didn't speak German well enough to talk to the internet installation customer-service people, rather than because I was a worthy intellectual who was too good for the internet at home. But it did mean that in the evenings when I went back to The Platz after work I couldn't call anyone on Skype or watch television. Sometimes I looked at my phone and sometimes I read books. Sometimes I worked on my writing. Sometimes I ate mango yoghurt from a jar and sometimes I sat listening to music on my phone and knitting a scarf that had no end.

When I was alone on weekends, I went out in the neighbourhood, or to a park, or swimming in a lake. I learned to cast my bikini off in best German naturist tradition and then panicked when the bottoms ended up buried deep in the murky silt. In Berlin my life felt quiet because I chose to make it so: because I did not know very many people, and because I did not understand German well enough to overhear passers-by unless I listened to them closely. For the most part, I chose not to. I relished the peace of my ignorance.

I had a beautiful bicycle named Judith. Judith was manufactured in Hungary and was solid and black and slow, with wire baskets in the front and in the rear. I parked

Judith in the courtyard of my building and most mornings I would ride Judith to the office and it was very charming, even though I had to ride for some time out of the neighbourhood over cobblestones that made Judith judder and my breasts shake up and down in my bra. I never wore a helmet when I rode Judith because that was not a thing that was generally done in Berlin.

On one particular morning in January I set out extra early, riding Judith to work. It was a perfect January morning: cold in a way that is befitting of January but warm enough to wear a winter coat and scarf and ride a bike. As I pedalled along I watched the neighbourhood come to life. People pushing their children in prams to their government-subsidized childcare. Business owners putting out folding chalkboards in front of their shops and restaurants. People wearing chunky knits with blankets wrapped around their knees drinking coffee and eating Brötchen at sidewalk cafes. If outside a Backerei a schnauzer had been standing in a nice sweater, playing a traditional German folk song on an accordion, I would not have been surprised.

This is so charming, I thought to myself as I cycled past these scenes. It's like I am living in a film, a charming film about my own life.

I crossed the road and left the cobblestones and started riding my bike down the bike lane on Kastianallee, a more serious and high-traffic Allee, down a hill towards Rosenthaler Platz. The wind blew in my face and then all of a sudden I felt something clunk on my head.

Fuck! I thought to myself, I think someone just threw something at me.

When I lived in London, this was not unusual: to ride my bike through a neighbourhood where women riding bikes were not entirely welcome, to be pelted with water balloons or eggs, trash heaved from a car window.

There are quite a lot of people in London who are assholes.

But there was something kind of sharp about the thing that the person threw at me as I rode down this hill in Berlin, and then I looked up and I saw that it was a bird and it had used my head as a helipad, taken a little pause on the top of my skull and taken off again.

The bird had ugly black feet. I watched it fly away and I tried not to fall off my bike and I did the only reasonable thing there is to do when you are reacting to a bird landing on your head while you are cycling down a hill: I screamed. I screamed and screamed all the way down to the corner, about five hundred metres or so, and then I pulled over and stood on the sidewalk and I laughed for about five minutes, doubled over my handlebars, tears streaking down my face. I'm sure that some of the passing-by Germans who were on their own charming commutes found me a little bit alarming.

That was how happy I was in Berlin.

It was the end of May in 2013 when my father's doctor started saying some of the things that doctors say in films, or in television series about hospitals where all of the doctors are having sex with each other. Phrases that are such a recognizable part of cancer narratives that when some-one says them in real life you might wonder, for a moment, if they're really being said. You might wonder if you're on camera. I wished that I was.

You'll want to organize your affairs, I was told the doctor had said to my father, and that she'd also said: Now would be a good time to do any travelling that you'd like to do.

Because I did not speak German well enough to talk to the internet installation customer-service people, I dis-cussed these things that the doctor had said to our father on a Skype call with Arthur at the end of a work day, when I was still in the office. My brother was at home in Califor-nia, nine time zones behind. He had called the doctor himself, to hear these phrases directly. I was not brave enough to do this. I needed him to be the conduit, to filter. I was sitting in a meeting room that was constructed from three pieces of glass and one solid wall. I sat with my back to the solid wall, as if that point of view would make me less vulnerable.

My brother and I discussed the implication of the phrases without saying the word that they implied.

What do you think I should do? I said to Arthur.

His wife was about to give birth to their second son. Our sister was living in Aberdeen in north-east Scotland with her husband. They had jobs at a university and were renovating a house.

You should probably move home, said my brother. Could you move to Baltimore? Or Washington, DC?

In another era, I thought, or in a Jane Austen novel, I

would be the spinster aunt, the eldest daughter doomed to always be alone in favour of looking after ageing parents.

No, I said to Arthur, I'm not going to move to Baltimore. But, I said, I could get my job to move me to New York. That way I'd be much closer, three hours on the train away instead of a many-hour flight.

That sounds like a good idea, my brother said.

It had never felt so hard before to leave a place. I loved Berlin. My one-way flight left early in the morning in late December. I used the local taxi app to call a cab at six o'clock in the morning. The day and night before I'd said goodbye to my friends, sent them away with my unwanted kitchen utensils, sat on the living-room floor and eaten a final falafel from the shop downstairs. On that final morning, in the cold and dark, I left the apartment, dragged my exploding duffel bags down three flights of stairs and across the courtyard of the building where I'd lived for a year, and paused in the graffiti-covered entryway.

The square was pitch dark and silent, but I looked around, just in case, for police. Out of my coat pocket I pulled a black Sharpie that I'd bought at a stationery shop the day before, for an express purpose. Amongst the multitude of scrawled and sprayed tags, I wrote my initials: JHE. I drew a heart after them. The taxi arrived. I got in.

Tegel, bitte, I said.

Wo ist dein Mann? the driver asked me: Where is your husband?

Nein, I said. Ich habe kein Mann.

But your husband called the taxi, the driver continued, auf Deutsch. Your husband, Jean. He used the app.

He pronounced my name as if I was a French man.

Nein, I said, kein Mann. Nein. Nichts. Genau.

It was too early in the morning to laugh.

Later I realized that the reason I left Berlin was to feel like I was doing something constructive in response to my father's diagnosis: I realized it a few weeks later when it became clear that my great dramatic act, my decision to cease my years of free living, had done nothing to reverse the course of the cancer. Of course it hadn't. But that didn't mean that in my subconscious, I had not tried.

I had never before felt anything but excited to leave a place that had become my home.

AFTER

1

In Baltimore, after my father died, in the weeks and months that followed, time disappeared, but also dragged. I was either in Baltimore or I was in Brooklyn. Sometimes I was on the train that goes between Penn Station in New York and Penn Station in Baltimore. I spent a thousand dollars on train tickets, or something like that. I chose not to do the math.

No matter the time of day, on every trip south I ate a toasted pumpernickel bagel spread with cream cheese. I bought the bagels from the deli in the bowels of New York Penn Station where I used to buy Dad's black-and-white cookies. On every trip north I ate peeled hardboiled eggs that came twinned in a plastic packet that burped a little bit of salt water when I opened it. I bought the eggs from the deli in Baltimore Penn Station, which was the only place to buy food besides a Dunkin' Donuts. This deli also had a bar, a desperate one. Each time I bought the eggs I thought: Should I also have a beer?

I never did. Which meant that when I took my eggs to go, I felt like I'd accomplished something. I felt like things could have been worse.

I had come back to America after fourteen years away, I was thirty-two years old, I was alone, and I was supposed to be building a new life in New York. But I wasn't trying very hard. All that late winter and early spring, after my father died but before my own diagnosis, most of what I knew in that country, my country, was a blur of trains and grief. At work, a consultant was brought in to help my team and to me she said: Tell your boss that you're ready to be back in the game! and I nodded as if I was. But I was just going to work to pay for my train tickets.

How long do you get to be sad about your father? I had no idea. In the office, I sat at my desk and re-read his obituary on the website of the Baltimore *Sun*.

When I was in Baltimore, my mother and I drank a lot of tea. I still didn't really like it, but I drank all that tea with my mother not for flavour, but for feeling.

Do you want a cup of tea? my mother would say, as soon as I arrived off the train from New York City, or when we got back to the house after going out to run an errand, or just in that stretch of afternoon between lunch and dinner. Before my father died I would often say: No, thank you, to the offer of tea. But after he died I would quite often say: Yes.

When I lived in England I drank a lot of tea, many cups a day, even though I didn't like it. I learned quite fast after I arrived in London that drinking tea was an important way to connect with people: when I went over to their homes, or if we worked together in an office. Being offered a cup of tea meant that you were being offered an entry to something, and accepting it was important.

I drank so much tea in London that I came to believe that I didn't mind the taste. I allowed my teeth to get a little yellow. But in Berlin, where it was not often offered, I'd realized that I wasn't that fond of tea, at least not when served according to the British custom. If I had a cup of tea after lunchtime it would almost always make me lie awake in bed until two or three a.m. But after my father died I almost always wanted tea with my mother, even if I just held the cup or sat next to it until it grew cold. Because making a cup of tea was a thing, under the circumstances, that my mother could do for me, or that I could do for her. It filled a space. It passed some time.

We drank the tea from mugs with various motifs that tracked the life of our family: decorated with logos from physics conferences, universities we'd attended, vacation spots we'd seen. We sat in the family room at the back of the house in Baltimore, and I always sat on the sofa, dark green with a small red print. My mother would sit across the room, in the reclining armchair that my father had spent so much time in, in the weeks and months before he died. The chair was also dark green, with a small red print, but if you looked close, the chair and the sofa did not match. My parents were not perfectionists. It's impossible to know what made their marriage work, of course, even as a witness to so many years of it, because what can any of us really know about a relationship that is not our own? But maybe their forgiving natures, their acceptance of good-enough upholstery, were among the things that made it possible for them to love each other so long and so much and so well.

I've made a decision, my mother said, from the reclining armchair. It was quite some time, and many cups of tea, since Dad had died, when she said this. In the initial days after his death, my mother kept repeating the advice that she'd been given by various people with recent knowledge of grief, people who'd lost their partners. They told her not to make any decisions too quickly, to wait a year before making a dramatic change. But now some time had passed and my mother was ready.

Oh? I said. Yes, my mother said, I'm moving back to Scotland. OK, I said. (What! I thought, I literally just left my life in Europe to be close you. LI-TE-RALLY.)

I'm sorry, my mother said.

It's OK, I said, I understand.

I did understand. I understood because my mother wanted to be near one of her children: of the three of us, my sister was the most settled.

I get it, I said, I would love you to move to Brooklyn, but I can't promise to be there in the long run.

I know, said my mother.

I also understood in a way that was harder to quantify, I suppose because I had grown up in America with my mother, and because throughout that young life my mother often referred to America as 'this country'. 'In this country', she said. It was not her country. My mother moved to America before I was born but did not become an American citizen until I was twenty.

When my mother told me that she was going to move back to the country where she was from, I also understood because I knew what it was to be a woman on my own and to do that.

Do you want to move back to Berlin? my boss asked me again, the first time I spoke to him after my father died.

We did not always get along, that boss and I, but he had worked hard to help me get back to America. He'd lost his father, too. No, no, I said, I'm glad to be here, in America.

My boss was not the first person to ask. Will you go back to Berlin? friends said, and I said, No, and sometimes I said: I feel sorry for my siblings, that they had to leave, to go back to their lives.

If I hadn't already moved back to America, I said, even if I still lived in Berlin, I don't think I would have been able to go back, when it happened. I think I would have abandoned my whole life there.

But of course I said that, because I didn't actually have anything to go back to. I had already abandoned my whole life there, disassembled my apartment, given away my possessions, posted a sign in the inner courtyard window of my living room that said: Tschussi, Nachbarn! so that the men making smoothies in their matching red tracksuits and the other neighbours who I'd watched for a year would know that I was leaving, and that I'd cared about them.

When I left Berlin, I felt pulled, reluctant, but I didn't feel like I could return. After the loss of my father I needed to be in the place where I'd come from. So I understood what my mother was doing, when she decided to move back to Scotland. But I was still sad.

There were ways in which my mother and I had sometimes been a little hard on each other over the years, as mothers and daughters can be. But after my father died, it seemed to me that we both set these ways aside, for the most part. We were both very kind. Whereas my siblings had partners, my mother and I were both on our own, and so we leaned on each other in a way that maybe we had never leaned on each other before. Instead of rolling my eyes and sighing, I waited for her when I felt that she was being too slow and deliberate. Instead of snapping at me for not paying attention, my mother kept quiet when she thought I was being careless and flip.

After the funeral, when my brother went back to his family in California, and my sister and her husband went back to Scotland, it was just the two of us left in Baltimore. Me and my mother and the things that my father had left behind. The cushions of his chair, still holding the shape of his body. A half-finished box of Kleenex. A half-finished book. Pain medications, wool sweaters, giant jars of raspberry jam that he had bought at the Russian grocery store that reminded him of his grandparents. A filing cabinet full of a lifetime of correspondence, from letters that my grandfather had sent him in the 1970s to emails from his children that he'd printed and put in a folder, for safekeeping. Magazines, photographs. Pairs of tweezers, pairs of socks. Loaves of bread he'd baked that were still in the freezer, still tasty when defrosted, sliced, and made into toast. Spread with jam.

A couple of weeks after my dad died, after my brother and sister had returned to their homes, my mother came upstairs to the guest room where I was skulking. I'd gone back to New York to move in to my new apartment and then I'd come back to Baltimore, to take care of my mother, or for my mother to take care of me. We never put words to which one it was. On that particular morning, my mother smiled and told me that my sister was on the phone and had some news for me. She handed me the cordless house phone, and I took it.

Elspeth said: I'm pregnant.

I said: Yes, I know. Then I handed the phone back to my mother.

I didn't know, not for sure, but I had suspected. I'd noticed that my sister did not drink any alcohol in the days when we were together just after Dad died, which seemed to me like a better time to drink than most. I had also noticed that she looked a little fuller than usual around her waist. That my sister had not only something to return to, a real home to go back to, after our father died, but had something to be happy about, that my sister was going to become a mother, was not something that I felt able to contemplate.

That my five-years-younger sister got married before me had not upset me.

But that she was going to have a baby, when I felt so hopeless and unmoored and alone: that was hard to take.

Before the death of my father, the last time my mother and I had spent so much time in each other's exclusive company I was in nursery school. It was before my sister was born, and when my brother was in school for six hours every day. I remember the joy of it: her reading me nursery rhymes aloud for hours, me playing in the kitchen while she talked on the rotary phone, riding in the shopping cart through the supermarket, watching through the bay window in the front of the house for the yellow school bus to deposit my brother at the end of his day.

But my mother sometimes recounted a story of an occasion in that era when I was very small and fell and hurt myself on the front steps of the house that we lived in then. I don't remember falling, but I do remember those front steps, which were cement and sharp-edged.

You were crying, my mother said, when she told me the story, which she did now and then. You were crying, and I tried to comfort you, but you pushed me away and went to your bedroom and climbed into bed and faced the wall.

When my mother told me this story, it made sense, almost as if I remembered it myself. I had always adored my mother, and she had always adored me, but I think sometimes I needed more space from her than she needed from me.

And then sometimes when she needed more space from me, I did not allow her to take it. Ten years or so later, when I was overcome with depression, my mother was my fiercest advocate. I remember lying on a rug in the kitchen with the family dog while she called adolescent psychiatrists, one after the other, trying to find one who would take our insurance and who would take me as a patient. My mother got me through that illness, and its relapses, with total focus and determination. I'm sure it was very hard for her.

But now, in this new stage of life in which we needed each other, my mother and I found ways to be softer and kinder. We solved problems together without raising our voices, or almost never. When we did, it was often because we were faced with the kinds of obstacles that we were used to having my father resolve: a broken dishwasher, a malfunctioning vacuum cleaner. We went to the movies together. We went out to dinner. We went to a wedding together because neither of us had an And Guest. We left the wedding early, went back to the Courtyard Marriott where we were sharing a room, and laughed at our nearly matching pyjamas: navy with small white polka dots.

On the occasion of the one-year anniversary of Dad's death, I went to Baltimore to spend time with my mother because I decided that she would need company, or maybe because I needed company, but either way I got so upset and angry – at my mother, but really at my father, at death – I decided to leave days earlier than planned. That was the worst time between us after Dad died, I think, the darkest time, but still, my mother and I soon found our way back together to a place we could share that felt loving and good.

My mother came to Brooklyn to see me for the first time a few months after I'd moved there, and a few months after Dad died. She helped me set up my new apartment, the one I'd chosen because I'd hoped he would be able to make it up the stairs. It was her birthday that weekend, and for the occasion I took her to a pizza restaurant with a live jazz band at the end of the block. The next day she bought me an end table with a ceramic top from a man across the street from my new apartment who was selling off a houseful of junk.

Afterwards my mother and I agreed that it had been

acquired by dubious means: that the man who sold it to us was not, as he claimed, a distinguished psychiatrist, selling a houseful of junk before using the building to set up his distinguished psychiatry practice.

That man, my mother said, is not a psychiatrist!

You don't think so? I said. I guess you may be right that psychiatrists don't usually have housefuls of antiques to sell before they can set up their private practices on obscure Brooklyn streets near the Brooklyn–Queens Expressway.

Definitely not! my mother said. That is not usual!

We laughed.

It's a nice table, I said.

I put the table next to an armchair in my windowless living room and my mother was the first person to set something down on it: her cup of tea, between sips.

I understood why my mother would want to move back to Scotland, her country. But I did feel worried about who would be there to look after me if I got cancer.

If.

When.

2

In New York, the medical appointments started after the diagnosis, after the phone call, after the chat about snorkelling and yoga. After the end of that part of my life where I had no particular idea about how I was likely to die. The appointments came one after another. Each appointment led to more appointments. Then came the voicemails, from the medical assistants. Give us a call when you have a moment, the assistants said. I'd leave my desk in the office and go and sit on a cold cement step in the emergency stairwell, because it was the only place to make a private phone call without being overheard by colleagues. I'd call the medical assistants back and my hands would shake and the medical assistants would say: You need to make another appointment, or We're just making sure that you're attending your next appointment. They would say these things to me as if they believed I was sick.

Thank you, I'd say, when these assistants called me, because they were just doing their jobs, but I resented having to say it. I was not grateful. Memory has always been my strong point: at work, I rarely write to-do lists. I just remember things. But now I found that I was confused about which doctors I had to see: where, when. I recalled when I tried to understand math in high school with my dad, when he told me that the problem with my inability to retain what I'd learned was that I wasn't interested. I wasn't interested in these doctors, either. I remembered the list that he kept on his iPhone, entitled Bill's Cancer. I made my own, logging physicians' names and office addresses, phone numbers and specialties. I called it Jean's Doctors.

The last time I'd seen a doctor in the United States, in my earliest twenties, I'd been on the health insurance that my father's job provided for our family. I did not know how to manage it myself. I had never encountered a medical bill. In England and Germany, health care was free, but I'd rarely seen a doctor. I was rarely ill, and when I was, the doctors seemed disinclined to help me, as if they believed that my American accent meant that I was soft, and grasping. One London GP responded to my request for a particular kind of steroids to help me with my asthma with: We don't do that in this country! In response, I cried. And every time thereafter when I visited that doctor's surgery I saw that there was a note at the top of my file that said: Patient is difficult.

In England, doctors hadn't seemed interested in me. Now, it seemed, they couldn't get enough. Every evening in the Clinton Hill apartment, the landlady left my mail on a polished occasional table in the foyer of the building: stacks of correspondence from my health insurers, annotated lists of things they'd paid for. THIS IS NOT A BILL was printed on the documents, but even though they weren't an immediate demand for money, the litany of charges still felt like a threat. It had been less than a year since I moved to New York, but I already felt like I'd forgotten what I'd hoped for when I moved there.

When I first learned that I had Lynch syndrome, I'd sometimes say to people, Of course I've had this since the day I was born. I just know about it now.

When I said this I would shrug, do a people-pleasing smile, because I wanted to make the people I said it to feel more relaxed and less afraid. It was hard to mention cancer in relation to myself without making people panicked or uncomfortable or upset. Nothing is different, I'd say, to make them feel better. But what I really wanted to say was: I wish I didn't know this.

Sometimes I looked out at the New York City skyline – I could see the Empire State Building from the very tip-top of my street in Brooklyn, when I was walking home from the subway stop – and think: What if I had stayed in Berlin and never found out?

And then I would think: I was happy in Berlin.

One time in Berlin I had tried to call a doctor, or maybe a genetics institute, some place I'd found and parsed on the internet, to talk about getting a test for Lynch syndrome. But of course I couldn't speak German well enough to explain what it was that I wanted. I had many friends by then who were fluent German-speakers. If I really wanted to do it, I could have asked them for help. Instead, I hung up the phone. I had tried.

Sometimes, in the weeks and months after I received the diagnosis, I would think about killing myself. Suicide was something that I thought about a lot when I was a teenager, a very depressed one, in the time before I started taking antidepressants, at just fourteen, and in the ebbs and flows since. Over the years my suicidal feelings and I had reached a kind of peaceful coexistence, and on the rare occasions that they bubbled up I knew it was because I was under stress, or sad, or I had missed an appointment with my therapist, or was about to get my period, and not because I wanted to kill myself, or was going to try. Maybe it's hard for someone to understand, if they've never thought: I should kill myself, that this idea could roll around in my head for all these years so much it became no more than an off-key hum. But over all that time I'd learn to understand the difference between those self-destructive synaptic snaps and what I really desired.

But the thoughts I had after the diagnosis were different: they were not the familiar urges. They were thoughts about how everything felt over when I was not yet sure if it had really begun. On those days, I would find it hard to get out of bed, and when I finally left to go to work, I would walk up the street to the bus stop chanting a mantra in my head: My life has value. My life has value. My life has value.

That autumn, a young woman with brain cancer was in the news because she had decided to move to Oregon to end her life under the state's assisted-dying laws. She was twenty-nine, and she was beautiful, and she'd been diagnosed with cancer less than a year after she'd gotten married, which was something the media liked to emphasize, as if the loss of her life wasn't already sad enough: a man loved her enough to marry her, but she was going to die, anyway. Was choosing to die. I thought about that young woman a lot. Every day when I got to work, I would sit at my desk and google the latest update. The updates were usually illustrated with two photos: one, from before she was sick, cuddling a puppy. One more recent, when her face was puffy from steroids, and the puppy was nowhere to be seen. When, at last, the young woman got the legal clearance she needed to die, and did so, I shed a tear for this person who I'd never met, and I thought: I get it.

3

After the diagnosis, my first doctor's appointment was with a geneticist. An expert in explaining to people who they are. I suppose if they made it their business, in theory a geneticist could tell you everything that's good about yourself: that you're likely to be a talented artist, that you'll run far and fast, that your bones are thick and strong and reluctant to snap, that your hair will always be luxuriant. But geneticists aren't in the business of bringing people good news. The bread and butter of the genetics business is to tell you what's wrong, the errors your parents wrote in your body the day that you were conceived, thanks to the errors their parents wrote for them. Their parents, before. Ad infinitum.

The geneticist I went to see was in a clinic on the Upper East Side, a salubrious neighbourhood that I'd spent little time in, because when I came to New York I decided that I was a Brooklyn person, not an Upper East Side person. I had friends who lived there, who encouraged me to check out the neighbourhood, to come and visit, to think about making the Upper East Side my home. But when I got out of the subway at 86th Street, I knew it was not for me. The storefronts were shining big boxes. The people were smooth and well-groomed. The Upper East Side seemed like a kind of tidy place for Americans who had their lives in order, which was not a kind of person who I was.

It was still September when I went to my appointment with the geneticist. It was still mostly warm, I still had a bit of a tan left over from Mexico. On my way to the clinic I watched women. On the Upper East Side, I observed, many of them were white and thin and wealthy: they wore large diamond engagement rings and yoga clothing, Lululemon sports bras and leggings and vest tops, at an hour on a weekday that was neither before or after work, which were the only hours when I went to yoga classes during the week.

This impressed me: the appearance that these women did not have work to do beyond honing their tiny, tight bodies, perhaps because of the people who had given them their large diamond engagement rings. I looked at these women and I imagined what my own life would be like, or could have been like. If I had come to New York City straight after university, if I had different aims, could I too have a large diamond engagement ring and a yoga mat under my arm, a low body-fat percentage and hair treated quarterly with keratin to smooth the curls? Could I live in a high-rise apartment with a doorman, where all the doorframes were straight-edged and the floors didn't slant, where the windows opened from side-to-side instead of up and down and where there were no mice at all? In this life with level edges, would I go out to yoga with my mat and my diamond ring, would I meet neighbours in the elevator who were off to walk their small clean white dogs? Would I nod and smile at the neighbours and say a brief hello, but take care not to get to know them on a deeper level, because I wanted my life to remain contained within straight edges and I'd understand that this was their desire too? If I had aimed to become this kind of woman: a thin, diamond, right-angle woman, would it have mattered that I would still have had – because I'd always had – Lynch syndrome?

It didn't matter. I'd made my decisions and now it was too late for that kind of life. I was too old to get that kind of diamond ring. I would never be that thin. No matter how much time I spent hanging around the Starbucks by the entrance to the subway at 63rd Street and Lexington Avenue, I would never be chosen by one of the men who facilitated the daytime yoga and diamond lifestyle. I would always need to continue working at a job in an office that I didn't care a great deal about because I needed to have health insurance. On my walk to the genetics clinic, I looked at those women who I would never be, and thought: Even though you are thin and wealthy, some of you will die of cancer before I do, and you don't even know that yet.

It was an ungenerous thing to think about strangers, but it was not untrue.

The clinic where the geneticist worked was named after a person who was a little bit famous before he got sick, but mostly famous because he died of colon cancer. The endowment of the clinic was a generous act on the part of his family, but while I sat in the waiting room, in another chair covered with plastic, I also thought that it was not very uplifting to name a clinic designated to help people with a particular disease after a man who perished from it. I know this is quite traditional when it comes to naming clinics and waiting rooms, to commemorate people who were vanquished by the thing that you're trying to fight, but that's just my opinion. I'm not at an expert at naming clinics.

I was surprised that the geneticist emerged from the corridor and fetched me himself, rather than sending an assistant, as if he considered me to be important. I was happy to see that he looked to be at least twenty years older than me. *Old enough to be my father*, I thought, not that I was looking for a replacement. It was a comforting contrast to my youthful gastroenterologist: I am as guilty as anyone of ageism, of wanting the people who deliver bad news to seem more seasoned than me.

The geneticist's hair was black and puffy and luxurious, in a style that I associate more with high-rolling men on Wall Street than with geneticists. But then, I had never before had a reason or occasion to meet a geneticist. I had only googled him. The internet said that this doctor was a leading expert in Lynch syndrome. That seemed good. He shook my hand and introduced me to a genetic counsellor, a woman who looked around my age. Maybe she was even a couple of years younger than me. Her hair was splendid, long and pale and shiny. It was the kind of hair made for an insouciant flip, if that's a thing you want to do. The kind of hair I've always dreamed of, but don't have, because my brown curls are another thing that I inherited from my father, from his side of the family.

This was not the kind of appointment where you take

your clothes off and are probed. Instead, this was the kind of appointment where you sit at a table and listen to experts tell you facts about your body, which to the experts is problematic, and which to you is the thing that holds you in the world. The geneticist and the genetic counsellor ushered me past the clinic reception desk, down a hall and into a small room with no windows and a surfeit of wooden chairs. The chairs were clustered in a haphazard fashion around a round wooden conference table. Somehow I ended up in the chair in the furthest corner, the chair that was the hardest to escape from. The geneticist and the genetic counsellor sat across from me, on the other side of the table. They smiled. They opened a folder that contained everything that they felt they needed to know about me. The folder was slim.

I felt outnumbered: by the chairs, by the professionals.

So, the geneticist said, glancing at the piece of paper at the top of the slim pile, you tested positive for Lynch syndrome? How did you know to get tested?

Lynch syndrome is not even that uncommon, it turns out. About one in four hundred people have Lynch syndrome. But it isn't common for people with Lynch syndrome to get tested for it before they exhibit any symptoms: most people with Lynch syndrome only find out they have it when they have colon cancer, when their cancer is biopsied.

My father had Lynch syndrome, I told the geneticist. First he had skin cancer that was related to Lynch syndrome, and then he got lung cancer, and I believe that his oncologist said that the biopsy from the lung cancer indicated that it was caused by the same gene. Even though lung cancer is a rare occurrence with Lynch syndrome.

OK, the geneticist said. But your father hasn't had colon cancer?

No, I said, he hasn't. He didn't have colon cancer. He's dead. He died in February.

I'm sorry, the geneticist said. My father died in February, too.

This really isn't about you, I thought.

But what I said is: I'm sorry.

The geneticist looked at me, and I looked at him, and for some reason I laughed, as if to say: Dads! What are they like? Dying in February!

When in fact what I was thinking was: Your dad was probably an appropriate age for a dad to die.

The geneticist moved on to explaining what kinds of cancer I'm at high risk of developing. It's a lot of kinds of cancer. An exhaustive list. Colon, oesophagus, stomach, pancreas. And because I am a woman: endometrial cancer. Ovarian cancer.

For women with Lynch syndrome, the geneticist said, the recommendation is a prophylactic hysterectomy.

I already knew this. This is the phrase that I had googled the most: prophylactic hysterectomy. I'd searched and re-searched it so often that for the first time in my life, I knew how to spell 'prophylactic' by heart. I looked at the geneticist.

I haven't had children yet, I said. I mean, I want to have children, but I don't have a partner.

The geneticist and the genetic counsellor looked at me.

I looked at the door to the room, which was between me, and them, and all the chairs.

To get out of this room, I thought, I would have to climb over all of these chairs.

No one said anything for a long while.

This, I thought, is the saddest silence of my entire life.

I'm not going to do that right now, I said.

I couldn't even say the word. I couldn't say: I am not going to have a hysterectomy.

OK, said the geneticist.

I nodded.

You know, said the geneticist, as if he was trying to lighten the mood, if you want to have kids, this is New York City, so you can have IVF! That's what women do here!

The kind of women he was talking about were not women like me: they were women like the ones I saw on the way to the clinic, the women with diamonds and husbands. Women who had clear plans for their lives. I was a little surprised that the geneticist hadn't noticed that I was not one of those women, but then again, the file of information that he had on me was only slim. It didn't tell him what my tax bracket was, or the extent of my loneliness.

You can test the embryos for Lynch and ensure that you only use the ones that don't have it, in order to eliminate the chance that you'll pass the disease on to your children! the geneticist said, with even more cheer.

Good thing for me that this was not an option for my parents, I thought.

I see, I said.

My mouth felt very dry.

Well, said the genetic counsellor, and to me she sounded disappointed, if we're not going to take your ovaries, then there are some gynaecological exams you can have, to screen for these cancers.

OK, I said.

The genetic counsellor frowned.

But they're not very effective, she said.

Her tone made me think that no one had ever tried to take her ovaries.

OK, I said, yes. I'll do those. I'll do the tests.

You'll also have a colonoscopy and an endoscopy, said the doctor. Mammograms, breast ultrasounds. And every year, an abdominal MRI. Your insurance might not cover that one, which is a shame, because it's very expensive!

I should get a family discount, I thought.

What else? the geneticist said. He paused. He furrowed his brow.

Brain cancer! the genetic counsellor said, in a tone that I found smug. You could test her for brain cancer!

Oh, OK, said the doctor. Shall I test you for brain cancer?

Sure, I said. Why not!

We climbed out of the tangle of chairs and walked across the hall into an examination room. I hopped up on the paper-covered table. The geneticist shone a light in my eyes, asked me to count backwards in sevens. He pounded my knees with a hammer. He told me to get off the table and walk across the room in a straight line.

Like you're a runway model! he said.

I stared at the wall, fuming. I was full of regret that I was wearing a somewhat figure-hugging dress.

I'm a fucking adult, I thought, but did not say.

You don't have brain cancer! said the doctor, after I walked.

I turned around.

Cool, I said. What are my chances of getting brain cancer?

Two to three per cent, the doctor said.

That didn't sound so bad.

Maybe, I thought, *maybe this is some good news, at last.*

I smiled.

What are the chances of brain cancer in the normal population? I said.

Much better, said the doctor. Like one in ten thousand.

Oh, I said.

My appointment was over. I agreed to return to see the geneticist the following year. The genetic counsellor handed me a list of the appointments that I needed to fulfil next. A checklist. I agreed to schedule an MRI, a colonoscopy, a mammogram. I agreed to see a dermatologist. I agreed to make an appointment with a special gynaecologist, a cancer specialist who would insert a thin steel rod through my cervix to scrape fresh cells off the walls of my uterus, to see if there was anything gestating there that would eat me alive.

I stepped outside, and gulped the air. I needed to go back to work, I had already missed several hours in the office. But I wasn't ready to be at my desk. Instead of getting on the subway downtown to Union Square, I decided to walk for a while. I headed south, along York Avenue. Medicine is the key industry in that far-eastern part of the Upper East Side. The blocks are full of hospitals and the businesses that support hospitals. There are healthcare supply shops where you can buy bandages, crutches, commodes. There are uniform stores where you can buy scrubs, white coats, rubber clogs. There are twenty-four-hour diners where you can eat bland, invalid-friendly food – clear chicken-based soups, tuna melts on white bread, milk puddings – while you gaze out a window and think about mortality.

I walked a couple of blocks further south and arrived at the Sloan Kettering Institute, one of the world's leading cancer hospitals, a series of huge grey cubes on either side of the street. They loomed.

I wonder if I will die in one of those buildings, I thought.

And then I decided I should stop thinking about that, so I turned away. I walked west, on 57th Street. I passed an old-fashioned wig shop offering a wide range of styles to suit all kinds of people who've lost their hair to chemotherapy. There was a luxurious updo in the centre of the front window, a swirl of grey strands caught up in a thick bun. It was displayed on a mannequin head that had the perfect sharp features of a Latvian mail-order bride. The head was on a turntable. The turntable moved clockwise, at a decorous speed.

I stood for a while at the window and watched the wig spin.

4

I began to enjoy living in New York. I found some space in myself to allow it.

I spent time with my old friends and made some new ones – people from work, friends-of-friends from London and Berlin. My job was busy and interesting and it gave me opportunities to travel: back to Germany, out to San Francisco. I settled in to my apartment: bought more furniture, hung more pictures in frames. I signed up for a seminar that was full of other people who were also a little adrift and hopeful that writing would give them more purchase or direction. I bought a second-hand bicycle from a woman who was returning to Sweden from Brooklyn, and I rode it in creaking circles around Prospect Park.

On the subway platform one warm evening I made eye contact over the edge of my copy of the *New Yorker* with a man who was reading a book of poetry and had a hard hat dangling from his backpack. He smiled at me. I smiled back. He looked like the man of my dreams. We exchanged glances until his train came and then, in an unprecedented act of boldness, I got on, too, even though it wasn't my train, and said hello, and gave him my business card.

This is me in New York, I thought in triumph, as I waved goodbye and got off at the next stop to switch to my correct train, this is the kind of woman I am in New York!

I never saw the man from the subway again: he texted me poetry for two weeks but cancelled two dates with excuses so preposterous that he had to be married. Still, I loved that it happened. It was a moment of organic romance. A good story. The kind of thing that is supposed to happen to a woman on her own in New York.

Friends came to town, from London, from California, from Boston. I showed them the small parts of the city that had become mine so far. I had a supermarket routine, a favourite spot for dinner and a favourite bookshop. I knew where to get on the Q train in the morning to be closest to the right exit in Union Square.

Brie came to town, on a work trip, we ate dinner at a gluten-free restaurant and then went to see a psychic. She suggested it. It was six weeks or so since my diagnosis, and it was a real comfort to see her: one of my oldest friends, someone I'd known since university, and through years of ups and downs in London. It felt safe to be honest with Brie about just how bad I felt. She'd seen me crack open before, after all, like the time a couple of years earlier when she sat with me on her sofa while I sobbed at an album of photos of her cousin's new golden retriever puppy.

We were on Third Avenue, somewhere in the east thirties, when we saw the sign for the psychic, outside a walkup apartment building, a grey and unprepossessing one.

Let's see this psychic! Brie said. It's only ten dollars!

I'm sure it's not really only ten dollars, I said.

Brie was already ringing the doorbell.

OK, I said.

Someone buzzed us into the building. We went up to the first floor, where the psychic was supposed to be, and waited. No one came to any doors.

You'd think they would know we were here, I said.

Finally, a man opened the door and looked at us. He turned around and said something in a language that I think was Romany, and then he was replaced by a young woman. She was maybe seventeen. She peered out at us from a dark room.

Just a moment, she said, I'm going to get the reader.

A minute later, she came back out, wearing a lavender bathrobe. She was the reader.

Come through here, she said, the usual reading room is not available.

She led us to the apartment next door, a studio, with a large grey sofa and a grey carpet and grey walls, and a coffee table with a shelf underneath that was exploding with unopened utility bills. There was a television on in the next room. I could hear a football game, and voices of men discussing the football game.

Brie volunteered to go first. The psychic analysed different parts of Brie's life.

Your career is not what you want it to be, the psychic said.

Actually, Brie said, I'm very happy with my career. In fact, I am doing the thing I wanted to do way back when I was in college!

I nodded. It was true.

Your love life, said the psychic, you're not sure about where it's going.

Yes, Brie said.

You are alone, said the psychic. You eat alone, you sleep alone, you wake up alone. I want to help you.

OK, Brie said.

I can light some special candles for you, said the psychic. They are spiritual candles. You can't buy them in a store. They are three feet tall. There are three. Red, for love, and green and gold, for money and business.

Oh, Brie said, well. The thing is, I am only in New York for forty-eight hours.

I want to pray for you, the psychic said, and light the candles. You just pay for the cost of the candles and you can donate any money you like for my time.

No, Brie said, I really just want the ten-dollar reading.

Money will come and go, said the psychic, and I can see that you will always have enough money. But this is your life. I want to help you with your life.

No thanks, Brie said.

One hundred and seventy-eight dollars, the psychic said. That's the cost of the candles.

I really don't want the candles, said Brie, but thank you.

She turned to me.

Jean! Brie said, in a bright voice. It's your turn!

She smiled at me. The psychic smiled at me.

Our friends, I said to Brie, we have to meet our friends!

I took a twenty-dollar bill out of my wallet and put it on the coffee table.

Thank you! I said to the psychic. I'm so sorry that we have to leave now to meet our friends!

Brie and I flew down the stairs and out on to the street, laughing with relief.

I did not believe in the psychic. I also did not want to learn anything more about my future. I felt like I already knew more than enough.

Seb was another friend from London. He moved back to New York for good about a year after me. We'd been friends since we were in our mid-twenties, ever since we were aspiring journalists in London trying to figure out what we were doing with our lives. We'd started on similar paths, working on the hipster magazine in Dalston. But then I stayed in London and Seb moved to northern Iraq, to live in Kurdistan and take photographs of war and peace and human joy and suffering.

He returned for reasons similar to mine: he grew up in the city, on the Upper West Side, and he came back because his mother, Joanna, was diagnosed with cancer. At first it was just a temporary measure, a visit to support her while she recovered from surgery. We met a day or two after she'd been discharged, at her apartment. Seb's childhood home. We all ate dinner together, but then Joanna went to bed early. The surgery was gruelling. A few days later, she'd learned that she needed chemo, radiation, too. A few weeks after that, Seb decided he didn't want to live in Iraq any more.

In her convalescence, Joanna was sleeping in Seb's old

room – the bed was lower, easier to get in and out of – so Seb and I reclined on her tall king-sized bed and whispered like teenagers at a sleepover, except that we were in our early thirties, and drinking glasses of good white wine from a bottle that we found in Joanna's fridge. There was a cold wind blowing outside, over the Hudson River, and Joanna's bed was stacked with many pleasant and luxurious pillows, the room hung with beautiful, tasteful art. It would have been a cosy scene if we weren't talking about heartbreak and death.

Seb was in the process of breaking up with the girlfriend he'd been in a relationship with for some time and we talked about that. It was always a long-distance relationship, always a little tricky to manage, but they had been devoted to each other, made it work. Until Seb went back to New York. When Seb went back to New York, it seemed like the girlfriend pulled away from him emotionally, even though he needed her more than usual, because of his mother's cancer. As we talked and drank more wine it struck me that Seb seemed stressed, by his mother's illness, but also distressed by his girlfriend's absence. I saw his distress and it occurred to me that perhaps having a partner to love and support you during times of personal crisis might not be as helpful as I had imagined, or hoped.

I'm sorry, Seb said, after a while, after we finished discussing the situation with his girlfriend, how it was at once unresolved and inevitable.

Sorry for what? I said.

That I wasn't around when your dad was sick, and

when he died. I'm sorry that I didn't realize what it was like. I'm sorry.

It's OK, I said.

It was. Seb and I had been friends for almost a decade after the fizzling of a brief romance of the kind you have when you're twenty-five and you meet someone and they seem interesting and you think, Hey! Might as well. It's rare that these liaisons end in anything but the imperative not to make eye contact when you pass in the street, but when our mutual ambivalences came to a head and I confronted Seb about it in the middle of a pavement in Finsbury Park, I said: Well, we can carry on like this and grow to hate each other, or we can stop now and be best friends for ever.

I choose best friends for ever, Seb said.

OK, I said, best friends for ever.

Then we shook hands.

Now, there we were on a cold night in his mother's apartment on the Upper West Side, and we were lying in bed drinking wine, and I was telling Seb about the prophylactic hysterectomy. It was still a hard thing for me to put into words, to say: Because I am probably going to get cancer, I am going to let a doctor take out my womb and ovaries.

I guess maybe I'll never have a baby, I said to Seb, which was something I had been thinking about a lot of the time, too, but had never said out loud. Until then, with him, I had just not allowed it.

I swallowed more wine.

I'll have a baby with you! Seb said.

Ew, I said, no way. We need to diversify our gene pools,

not have kids with other Jewish people who are bound to get cancer!

Seb frowned. He looked a little insulted.

That's what caused all of these problems in the first place! I said. Jewish people! Having babies with other Jewish people!

I feel like I'm in a Woody Allen movie, Seb said.

I felt a little bit less alone.

5

The ultrasound clinic was also on the Upper East Side, but the waiting room was far brighter and cheerier than the other ones that I had encountered in the time since my diagnosis. The receptionists were smiling. The magazines were about fashion and parenting, and arranged in straight lines. The room was decorated in shades of blush, and not named after a dead person. The chairs were upholstered with fabric that indicated that the person making the design decisions was not preoccupied by concerns that the chairs would be sat in by people who had faecal incontinence.

It was a room filled with people who were waiting for joy. The other women in the room with me were there because they were pregnant, not because they were trying not to die. They were also all accompanied by men. I was the only person sitting alone. The women were all wearing wedding and engagement rings and the men were all looking at iPhones. To be fair, the women were all looking at iPhones, too. I was also looking at an iPhone. There was a lot of love in this room, between the pregnant women and the fathers of their babies, sure, but there was also a lot of love for iPhones.

This ultrasound of my uterus and ovaries was one of

the exams that the genetic counsellor had told me was not very effective. Not as effective as having a hysterectomy. But I was willing to try. In part because I had a desire to prove the genetic counsellor wrong. But mostly because I wanted to keep my ovaries and uterus inside my body. I wanted to keep bleeding every month. Now, each box of tampons that I bought became an act of defiance. Now, my period was less of an inconvenience, more of an assertion that my body was still whole and still mine. I relished the sight of the blood.

It was nine o'clock in the morning when I arrived for the ultrasound and I was tired. I had flown back from a work trip to Europe the night before. I was exhausted from jet lag, and hungry because I had not eaten breakfast: because I didn't have time, or wasn't organized enough, or was too anxious to eat. One of those. To get to the appointment, I took a cab from my apartment in Brooklyn all the way to the clinic in Manhattan. This cost me about $50, and took an hour, but I did it anyway, because I could not make my body rise in time to take the subway, or because I could not make my body get on the subway. I needed to put the responsibility for moving my body from home to clinic into the hands of a man who was behind the steering wheel of a car that I summoned with an app on my phone. I could not do that on my own.

In the waiting room, my stomach growled. I fished around in my handbag to see if I had any snacks. The bag was large, and full of detritus from my long-haul flight the day before. I dug through subscription cards that had fallen out of the magazine I'd been reading, the stub of my boarding pass. A crumpled napkin from the Pret a Manager in Heathrow Terminal 5, smudged with lipstick and what was once the foam of a soy latte. I located a packet of individually-wrapped boiled ginger sweets that I had eaten on the plane to pass the time. One an hour, then two. There was a single sweet left at the bottom of the packet. I smiled.

I pulled the sweet out of the bag, and unwrapped it with the hand that was not holding my iPhone, and because I only had one available hand the sweet slipped out of the wrapper too fast and fell on the tasteful carpet of the clinic waiting room. I looked around the room to see if anyone noticed the sweet bouncing on the floor. I was very hungry. Everyone was still gazing at their iPhones, as if they were practising what it would be like to behold and love the babies whom they were in this ultrasound waiting room to admire. I picked the sweet up off the floor.

I guess if these people think I am pregnant and see me eat this sweet that I have dropped on the floor, I guess they might think I will be a terrible mother, I thought.

Then I ate it.

The room in which I had the actual ultrasound exam seemed fancy to me. But there were things that fanciness could not ameliorate: I still had to pull on a hospital gown. I still had to lie back on the examination bed and put my feet in the stirrups.

The exam was a transvaginal ultrasound. Hello, said the ultrasound technician, in a monotonous voice, and inserted the wand inside me. That was a bit of a shock. Before I came in for the appointment, I had googled the

procedure on the internet. Of course I had: just like I googled all my appointments. When I googled, I discovered
radical feminist health forums that argued that transvaginal ultrasounds are in themselves a kind of sexual assault,
a form of forced penetration. The forums suggested that
women should be able to refuse internal ultrasounds as a
matter of feminist practice, as an assertion of being in
charge of their physical selves.

What is the word for when someone penetrates you
without your enthusiastic permission, but where you feel
in one way or another complicit, or at least resigned? This
hospital examination room is not the only place where it's
happened to me. I'm not unusual. Like many women I've
had times in my life where I've gone to bed with men willing to participate up to a line that a man then decided to
cross. I'm not unusual to have decided afterwards to accept
some culpability, to think I have only myself to blame,
rather than to consider the implications of having been the
victim of an act of betrayal of trust. Men whose attention
to what I desired was strong but then, when it was most
important, vanished.

Most of the time I'd find ways not to think of those
men, to forget about them. But I thought of them now,
during this exam, because it reminded me: because this
penetration did not feel like something that I wished for,
but it also didn't feel like something that I had the ability
or agency to refuse.

The technician said nothing while she moved her wand
around. I winced: once, twice. Again. The technician typed
on a keyboard with one hand. She clicked on the screen

with her mouse and typed some more. I looked up at the monitor. The images looked familiar: just like the ones that popped up quite often in my Facebook feed. Images posted by women I hadn't seen since high school, or who I'd worked with for six months, or who I'd met one time years ago at a party. On occasion, the images were posted by men. The images I saw on the screen reminded me of them, except that in this case, the uterus was empty.

Would it be funny, I thought, if I posted these ultrasounds on Facebook?

I decided it would probably not be funny.

The ultrasound technician removed the probe and left the room to show the images to a radiologist. You can sit up, she said, in her monotone voice, as she left, but don't get dressed.

I sat up. I didn't get dressed. I had been to many appointments and I had become good at following instructions. At one of the appointments, there was a poster on the wall, an image from a breast cancer awareness campaign. As I sat there in an ugly hospital gown, waiting for a pathologist who'd stabbed a small lump in my right breast with a needle to finish looking at her slide in order to tell me whether or not I had breast cancer, I looked at the poster and thought: Guys, I could not be more aware.

(It was an insect bite, it turned out, in the end. Benign, the pathologist said, and I repeated it in my head as I walked out of the clinic and the few blocks back to work, as if it was the most beautiful word in the world: Benign, benign, benign.)

As I waited for the results of the ultrasound, again

alone, again wearing an ugly hospital gown, I wondered: Is it odd that I always come to these appointments on my own, that I always spend these blank times waiting to hear if I have cancer without anyone to hold my hand?

But I didn't know who to ask: there was no one with any obligation. After my diagnosis, my mother had written me an email saying: I will come to New York to go to your appointments with you, and I knew that she meant it, as long as she lived in Baltimore.

But it seemed like too much to expect her to travel to New York from Baltimore each time yet another part of my body was being examined. I had close friends in New York – Seb, Kylah, others – but how do you get someone to rearrange their weekday schedule to sit in a clinic waiting room just in case you have cancer, when you have to come to these clinics again and again and again? When every week you might have cancer? I did not want to waste anyone's time. I also did not want to make a fuss. A fuss might be a problem for other people. It might mean that I really had a problem.

They didn't leave me waiting as long at the ultrasound clinic as they had at the breast surgeon's, which meant that the ultrasound technician returned before I'd had time to think about the things I usually considered in these situations: what poems should be read at my funeral, and also whether poetry was a thing I would have time to become interested in while dying.

He doesn't need to see anything else, the ultrasound technician said.

The he that she was referring to was the radiologist.

Her voice was still so flat and affectless I wondered: What does it sound like when you deliver news that is not good?

But no matter. On that particular day, it was not my job to find out.

The MRI came next. This time, I didn't notice the state of the waiting room because I was too busy being afraid. I was more frightened of going in the MRI tube than I was frightened of cancer. This was maybe odd because my father had been one of the people who had invented the tube. This was also maybe odd because I was going in the tube to see if I had cancer. But it was not odd because I knew that I was definitely going in the tube, and after all those exams I had begun to think it was unlikely that I had cancer.

I remember feeling real panic in a small space for the first time when I was ten, at the Smithsonian, in the American History Museum. We were on a family vacation to Washington, DC, walking up and down the Mall on a warm spring day. It was raining, suddenly, so everyone poured in from the open green space to seek shelter, and at some point the First Ladies exhibition was so packed that I got squashed – just ten years old, still less than five feet tall – against the glass of a case that contained a sparkling evening dress once worn by Nancy Reagan. From that day forward, I always looked for exit routes, often cried without consolation when flying on a plane.

When I was a teenager, my father and I would often stop by his laboratory after we'd finished running errands on a Saturday or a Sunday afternoon: I'd zoom up and down the shiny hall floors in a rolling desk chair while my father caught up on his work. On one particular day, I don't remember when, on the way into the building, I remarked that I could understand why, when my father told people what he did for a living, that he worked on the development of MRI, they often said: It's so claustrophobic!

I was at that age, I guess, when you say things to your parents to show that you are prepared to challenge their beliefs.

It really looks claustrophobic! I said to my father, about the tube.

Get in, my dad said, and I climbed up on the tray and he put me in the MRI tube as if I was being scanned.

OK, I said.

This is what it's like when they scan your back, he said, and then he made the tray bring me further back into the tube.

It's not that bad! I said, because I knew if I said that he would take me out. He did. Then we went to the supermarket together, and then we went home, where, with my mother, we drank a cup of tea.

But my time in the tube under the watchful eye of my father was not a cure for the feelings that I had in small spaces. As I grew older, the claustrophobia got worse. It got so bad that I balked and had a panic attack and got off a plane before it took off: once, then twice. When I was nineteen, my dad paid for the cognitive behavioural therapy I needed to get over my fear of flying. At the sessions the therapist taught me how to moderate my breathing to reduce my heart rate. She talked to me about the reasons that I was really afraid of flying: because I didn't want to be in a small space, because I didn't want to feel like I was not in control. To test me, she shut me in a small bathroom with the lights turned off.

How are you doing? she called. I was sitting on the linoleum, looking at the light that was coming through the gap at the bottom of the door.

Fine, I said, I am not afraid of bathrooms.

I guess it was ironic that I was on the verge of having a panic attack on my way to my first MRI because I was being scanned in a machine that my father partially invented, because of a gene that I inherited from him. Ironic that he could save my life from this gene he gave me, even though he was already dead. I thought about saying this to the MRI technician, telling him how ironic it was, but the man running the test was not very talkative. I decided to keep the thoughts to myself.

Instead, I climbed up on the tray that was like the one in my dad's machine all those years ago. The technician put a pillow under my head. He put foam earplugs in my ears and prodded with his fingers for my hipbones. He was rough. I need to find your pelvis, he said, after he had already started the prodding. I felt less upset than I once would have. By now I had crossed that Rubicon of healthcare where you come to understand that in certain contexts your body becomes a faulty object that must be prodded. By now I had learned to choose my battles.

The technician retreated into the control room. When the tray moved back into the tube, I closed my eyes and recalled what the therapist taught me to do all those years earlier when I was trying to get back on a plane. In the tube, I breathed in on a count of eight and out on a count of eight, and then I did it again. I did it again and again, and then even though I knew it was not a good idea, I opened my eyes. There was a thick stripe of glossy grey paint above me, down the middle of the empty whiteness of the tube, I think to define a depth of field for the patient's eyes. The stripe helped the tube feel more like a space and less like the blankness of death.

The tube was a bit shorter than the ones in the machines my father worked on twenty years earlier, and I realized that if I moved my head a bit, tipped it forward and back, I could see the room at either end. I was not in a coffin. I was almost relaxed. A switch was flicked and the ratatatatataatat began, still loud through the earplugs. When my father died, even on the actual day that he died, he was working on an experiment to make the machines quieter. I stared at a flaking blister in the grey paint. It had been a while since I cried about him, because crying on my own felt worse than being on my own but not crying. I'd learned to control it. But now, in the tube, as I lay still, my eyes welled up. I thought: Oh, Dad.

6

Around that time, I decided to start having sex. Or, to make an effort to have sex. I decided to start having sex because I suspected that when I had a hysterectomy, I might lose the desire to have sex. I suspected that when I had a hysterectomy, I might lose the appeal that I had to men. I suspected that it is problematic to be a single woman in your thirties because men assume you are desperate to have children, but even more problematic if you are facing surgery that is going to make that impossible. I also suspected that all of this is moot because these are not the kinds of conversations that you should have with a man unless he loves you very much. Being loved very much by a man was a thing that had not happened to me for a long time. I had a degree of belief that it would not happen again: that I should not expect it. I decided, instead, to have sex.

I was not very promiscuous, by nature or habit. When I decided, in this strange and sad time of my life, that I should be having more sex, it was counter to my previous belief that I should eschew sex unless I was having it with someone who I thought could love me. It contradicted my previous understanding that sex was something that I should try my best to withhold unless I was certain that the person I was having it with would offer me some kind of security.

The guilty way that I thought about sex was probably similar to many women my age who grew up in middle-class mostly-white mostly-Christian suburbs in the late 90s, who turned eighteen around the time Bill Clinton was impeached for getting a blow job from Monica Lewinsky. We disapproved of Monica Lewinsky. We disapproved of premarital sex. We didn't really know what blow jobs were. We'd heard rumours. Which is to say that it took me many years to feel OK about the fact that I could choose to have sex and enjoy sex and not feel bad about my desire for sex. Which is to say that even now, in my early thirties, I was still a bit afraid of having too much sex, of being a slut.

I learned at an early age that women who really enjoyed sex, who weren't neurotic about sex, were women who were not entirely deserving of love. It took me many years to unlearn that. In my early twenties I thought it was probably OK to have sex as long as I was already in a Serious Relationship with someone, and in my middle twenties I hoped that having sex would lead to someone deciding to be in a relationship with me, and for a while in my late twenties and early thirties, when I was not in a relationship, I decided to just have sex when I felt like it, though afterwards I often felt that maybe that was the wrong decision. For a time before I moved to New York I decided that perhaps I should revert to my earlier strategy, to hold back on having sex with a man until I met one who gave me the confidence that he loved me. This meant that I was celibate for quite a long period of time. During that time one of my friends asked me what my most beloved sexual fantasy was and I said: To have sex with someone who loves me! and oh, how we laughed, as if that was witty, and not just very true.

I decided to start having sex before I stopped having the desire for sex, before men ceased to desire me, before I needed to dig deeper into the article about sex after a hysterectomy that explained the ways and means to keep wanting it after all. I decided to start having sex because for now my body was still something that I had the ability to make decisions about.

I met Henri around the time I made that decision. Or maybe I made that decision around the time I met Henri.

I went on my first date with Henri one evening just a few hours after I'd arrived home from a business trip, back to my old office in Berlin. That morning, before I left the hotel to go to Tegel to catch my flight to New York, feeling sad about the life I'd left behind in Berlin and the one I hadn't quite figured out in Brooklyn, I lay in my big hotel room bed on my own and listened to a couple having sex in the room next door to or above mine. The woman was moaning with rhythmic pleasure.

That sounds nice, I thought, and maybe that's what I was still thinking that evening, when I went out to meet Henri for a drink. I was wearing the same figure-hugging dress I'd had on when the geneticist checked me for brain cancer. On my way out of my apartment I ran into my landlady, and she saw me in my figure-hugging dress and she said: You look nice.

So I guess that when I met Henri, I believed that I

looked nice. Henri did not tell me that I looked nice, but he was French, and he was handsome, and he had an extremely worthy and interesting career. Maybe Henri looked like Ryan Gosling, or maybe I had watched a movie starring Ryan Gosling on the flight back from Berlin. Either way, Henri and I met at a bar a few blocks from his apartment to drink whiskey. I was exhausted from my trip, so maybe I lost my inhibitions faster than I usually would, or maybe that's just an excuse. The next morning, when I walked out of Henri's apartment, I deleted his number from my phone, and decided that the reason that I had just slept with him was that I was jetlagged. I decided that the reason I had just slept with Henri was he had plied me with whiskey, and because Henri had an alluring French accent. But the truth was that I did it – went home with a man I did not know, had sex with him – because soon I might have a hysterectomy. Because soon I might have cancer. Because waiting to have sex with a man who loved me could mean that I might never have sex again. Because for now, for the time being, my body was still intact, and my own. I'm sure Henri would not have slept with me if he had known any of that.

I guess this is what a one-night stand is like, I thought to myself, as I got into the Uber that I'd summoned with my phone as I descended the stairs from Henri's fourth-floor walkup. Before I went into Henri's apartment, on the street outside the building he lived in, I demanded that he show me his driver's licence, as if knowing his middle name and date of birth would deter him from killing me. Even though nobody knew where I was. I took the car home, I showered and dressed and took another car to the office, so that I wouldn't be late, so that I wouldn't be wearing the figure-hugging dress yet again. So that I would give the impression that nothing out of the ordinary had happened, as if it was something anyone could detect. I deleted Henri's number from my phone that morning, when I walked out of the apartment, because I had no expectation that we would see each other again. Maybe because I wanted to ensure it.

But he texted me later, or the next day, something about how it was nice to meet me. How he had fun. I'd deleted his number but of course I knew at once that it was him.

It was nice to meet you, too, I wrote.

I added his number to my phone again. I saved his name as 'French'.

Henri was the kind of man I thought I wanted to be with, in various ways. He was tall, he was good-looking, a few years older than me. He was very intelligent, he worked for the UN in a job that meant that quite often he left New York to travel to dangerous locations that had been ravaged by war and natural disasters, in order to make them less ravaged. From what I could tell, Henri was kind of heroic, but it really was hard to tell, because Henri gave very little away. I didn't know about his family or his friends, except that he had them, and I didn't ask him many questions: because he didn't want to be asked, or because I didn't want to know. Henri had lived in his apartment for a few years but the decor was still sparse, perhaps because he travelled so much or perhaps because that's the kind of man Henri was. I didn't know. I noticed one picture tacked up on the wall, the only hint in the space of him as a person with tastes besides a box of cereal on his kitchen counter. The picture was a drawing of a nude woman with her back turned to the artist, in a position that was maybe supposed to represent a bit of light bondage. Henri didn't tell me about it, and I did not ask him.

I did tell Henri the first time that we met that I moved to New York because my father died and he said, I'm sorry, in a way that seemed polite but not interested. Henri was only interested in my body: he was very interested in my body, and he seemed to be uninterested in about everything else about me, expect when he perceived that his lack of interest would obstruct his access to my body again. This didn't matter to me. In fact, I think it was what I wanted, since everyone else with access to my body was focused on cataloguing its flaws.

His texts were always brief. We didn't chat. We didn't exchange jokes. I didn't tell Henri that I wasn't sleeping well these days. I didn't tell Henri about the doctors who kept telling me to remove my organs. I didn't tell Henri how I wondered about whether I would still be a woman after those parts of my body were removed, even though I believe that the state of being a woman is not exclusively determined by the physical body.

Sometimes I wondered what more was going on with Henri, why he seemed so closed and blank. I wondered if he had some kind of post-traumatic stress from one of the bad things he'd witnessed in one of the dangerous places he'd been, doing things that were probably heroic. I didn't ask. I knew that it was important not to discuss anything pertaining to feelings with Henri because if we started to know things about each other we would almost certainly stop sleeping together. That was not what I wanted from Henri, and not – I suppose – what he wanted from me.

Sometimes, after we had sex, which was always very good sex, I would pause for a moment before I put my clothes on. I would look at the ceiling and Henri would look at the ceiling, we'd leave a polite space on the fitted sheet between us, and I would think: *Man, is this guy dead inside or what!*

I didn't tell Henri that I had never thought too much in the past about whether I wanted to be a mother, and that now I thought all the time about my fear that I wouldn't be one. I didn't tell Henri about how some time ago I had decided that I would be more discerning about who I slept with, about how I had made a decision that I would not go to bed with a man who didn't care about me, and how that had led to a long period of celibacy, well over a year of celibacy, until I learned how my body's future betrayal of me was written in my DNA. Having sex with Henri was one way of saying that what those people had written in my body was not important. It was a way of saying: No: my body is mine.

I didn't tell Henri anything, not really. Not that I can recall. But every two weeks or so, my phone buzzed with a text from him. He would ask me to go for a drink, we would arrange a time to meet, and then we would go back to an apartment, mine or his. After a while we stopped going for a drink. After a while we'd just meet at his apartment or mine, chat about things like the weather and business travel for ten or fifteen minutes, and then we'd go to bed. After the first or second time, we stopped spending the night. One evening I drifted off for a moment and when I woke he had moved to the living room, still naked. He was sitting on his futon, watching YouTube videos on his laptop.

C'est horrible, I thought.

I'm going, I said, rising from the bed, pulling my clothes on, calling an Uber.

Henri got up from the futon, walked with me to the front door of the apartment. He kissed me goodbye with what felt like more affection than usual, which is to say any affection at all. I assumed it was because he was grateful to me for leaving. As I walked down the stairs of his building I felt more disgusted with myself than I usually felt after sleeping with Henri, which was always a little bit disgusted. I thought to myself as I walked down the stairs: *Never again*. It wasn't the first time I'd thought this after sleeping with Henri, but this time I thought it with more intent.

Once again, I deleted the listing for 'French' from my phone, but that didn't matter: Henri's number became the only one besides my mother's that I knew by heart.

Oh, I'd say to my friends, with a shrug, when they asked me about the state of my romantic life, I have a lover, he's French.

My friends seemed impressed. I didn't tell them about the incident with YouTube.

The stretches of time between our meetings grew longer. I assumed this was because Henri was dating someone more seriously. I wondered, for a moment, if he'd had a girlfriend the whole time. I didn't care. I went on dates with other men. One used my time to tell me the plot of the television series that he was writing.

I can tell you about all the episodes, he said, I have them all plotted out.

OK, I said, because I had nowhere else to go, and half a glass of wine left.

I went on a date with a Ph.D. student whose physical resemblance to a university ex-boyfriend repulsed me.

Want to kiss? he said.

No, I said.

I went on a date with an emergency-room doctor who met me for brunch after his overnight shift and got angry when the waiter wouldn't bring him wine.

This is a shitshow! the doctor said, in a loud stage whisper, and the waiter looked at me with great sorrow, assuming the doctor must be my horrifying alcoholic boyfriend.

I just smiled. I was happy that this was another man who didn't mean anything to me.

One day, after the longest period of silence ever, a couple of months, I got another text from Henri. Sorry I haven't been in touch, he wrote, as if he had failed to meet some expectations.

Nice to hear from you, I wrote, with no exclamation mark.

I want to take you to dinner, Henri responded.

Oh no, I thought, this will really be the end. But I texted him back: Yes.

I wanted to see what would happen.

We went to dinner, to an Italian restaurant near Henri's apartment in the West Village, just down the block. I suggested it because I'd been there before, on a date with another man, and I knew that the food was good and simple.

That's convenient for me, Henri texted when I suggested it.

Of course it was. I also suggested the restaurant because it was convenient for him. Because I wanted to sleep with him again but I also did not want him to come to my apartment again.

We sat outside. Other times, Henri had met me in my laziest clothes, my home-only sweats, but tonight I made an effort to wear a nice dress. Henri was wearing the sweater he wore on our first date. Maybe it was his best sweater, or the sweater he wore when he was trying his best. We ordered pasta.

Henri pronged a gnocchi with his fork.

Henri and I have slept together many times, I thought, but I have never before seen him eat.

We tried to make conversation, which also felt unfamiliar. Henri described a film he had watched on one of his long flights back from being heroic in a dangerous part of the world, an animated film, one that I hadn't seen because I dislike animated films, and never watch them.

It was cute, Henri said.

I tried to smile. I tried to still find him attractive. He does have a lovely face, I thought, and I still like his accent.

We held hands under the table, as if it would have mattered if someone saw us together. Maybe it would.

By then I already knew that we had ruined whatever it was that we once shared. But we stuck with our shared, unarticulated agenda. We went back to Henri's apartment. We had sex, but it wasn't good, not like it was before. Henri was frustrated. Maybe even a little angry. I was distracted and impatient. As we went through the motions together, I wasn't so sure that this was my first choice of things to do with my body, in that time and place. I'd guess that it wasn't his, either.

I put my nice dress back on when it was over. We said goodbye. It was awkward. This time Henri did not walk me to the door.

I knew it, I thought as I walked down the stairs, I knew that we should not have had dinner.

Once again, there was a car waiting to drive me back to Brooklyn. I climbed into the backseat. It was a relief.

Did you have a good night? the driver said.

Sure, I said. Sure. How's yours?

7

I was longing for someone to hear my colonoscopy joke. Friends who knew that I was going in for the procedure texted me that morning to wish me luck, so I used the joke then.

How are you feeling? my friends wrote.

This is the first time in my life that I haven't been literally full of shit, I wrote back.

Some of my friends responded. Haha, they wrote. Some of them just didn't respond. I tried not to judge the ones that I did not hear back from. Not too much.

The day before the colonoscopy, I was instructed, I should mix and consume a gallon of laxative solution in order to flush out the contents of my colon. At the gastroenterologist's office, a receptionist handed me a jug and an envelope of powder. In addition to the laxative, the instructions continued, I was permitted to consume only clear liquids: apple juice, black coffee, Jell-O. I went in and out of all of the bodegas in my neighbourhood looking for Jell-O that was not red, because red Jell-O was forbidden. I thought about my dad, and the tubs of Jell-O that he gave as gifts to neighbours, during his Jell-O phase. I thought about how if my dad was still alive, he would have made me Jell-O himself, green or yellow, presented with a flourish in a plastic tub that had once contained margarine.

I thought about how much I missed my dad.

I thought about how red Jell-O was clearly the preferred Jell-O in my neighbourhood.

This is a good time to live alone, I thought the night before my colonoscopy, each time I chugged back another glass of the laxative and each time I flushed, but really I wished that there was someone there to hold my hand and decant the gallon into a glass. To be obligated to pick me up from the clinic after the procedure. You're not allowed to go home on your own after a colonoscopy, because of the sedative. I didn't want to ask my mother to come to Brooklyn, because of the fuss. Henri was out of the question. One of my friends said she'd like to, but she was too busy with work. Another was out of town. These refusals felt more painful, perhaps, than they should. In the end, my friend Zoe agreed to help.

I let the receptionist at the colonoscopy clinic know that I'd arrived and she said, Did you drink a laxative? and I said, Yes, and then she said, We'll need a urine sample and I said, That will be a bit difficult because I haven't consumed anything since midnight, in accordance with your instructions!

I was cranky, and dehydrated.

The receptionist just looked at me and handed me a bracelet for my wrist. She gave me the kind of soft ridged plastic cup that you might use to get a drink of water from an office water cooler. It seemed a bit casual and unprofessional, for a urine sample.

The bathroom is over there, said the receptionist. We don't need much.

I walked to the bathroom and peed in the drinking cup and then carried the cup, hot and sloshing, but with not much, back through the waiting area, which was enormous. The waiting area resembled a bus station filled with dozens of people who were waiting for a bus going to a place they didn't want to go to. And who had all been drinking laxatives.

I'm done, I said to the receptionist. I held out my plastic cup of pee.

Oh, said the receptionist, oh, and I thought that probably she shouldn't touch it without gloves, but then instead of taking the container from me she summoned a colleague and the colleague escorted me back through the bus station, and through a sort of bus station anteroom, to another room where there was a big plastic bin.

Well, I thought, as I walked, well! Here I am, walking past dozens of strangers, holding an open cup of my own urine.

I set my cup in the big plastic bin. It was the only cup. It seemed strange, so unsanitary, so I looked it up on my phone when I got back to my seat in the bus station. It was a pregnancy test, of course. You can't have a colonoscopy if you're pregnant. Mine was the only drinking cup of pee because most of the people in the bus station were well into their fifties, or men, or both.

I was not pregnant.

At last, it was my turn. A nurse called my name and beckoned me from the bus station into a windowless room with an accordion door made out of a material that was just a step up from cardboard. She handed me a gown, a voluminous no-colour thing.

Change into this, she said, you can leave your T-shirt on, and your socks.

I put my arms through the gown like a pre-school art smock, and then fashioned the remaining billowing fabric into a sort of wrap dress in the style of Diane von Fürstenburg.

I took off my sweatpants, my underwear, and put them in a plastic bag that I hoped would be returned to me, not to another person waiting in the bus station. I sat, and waited, and then the accordion door started pulling back and I thought, Aha! It's my turn! but the person pulling the accordion was an elderly man who was also waiting for a colonoscopy. He seemed confused. I looked at him and he looked at me, we were both wearing the same wrap dress, and then he staggered back into his own cardboard-doored area.

In time an anaesthesiologist showed up. He stuck an IV port in my arm. Weeks later, I got a bill for $7000 from this anaesthesiologist. When I protested the bill, the office told me that the doctor charged me because he didn't accept my insurance.

You should have said something, the anaesthesiologist's secretary said, in an accusing tone.

I was literally asleep, I replied.

Wrap this blanket around your waist, the anaesthesiologist said, handing me one.

And I did so, obedient, even though there was no

chance that I was going to flash my bum at any of the other colonoscopy patients in the voluminous gown. Even though if I did expose myself to any of the other colonoscopy patients, I'm sure they would have observed it with nothing more than a frisson of empathy. We were all in this together, having cameras shoved up our asses.

In the procedure room I lay down on the bed and assumed the required position, which was on my side and involved straps and felt like the precursor to something sexually humiliating. My old pal the gastroenterologist entered the room.

Hello, he said, and then he stroked my hair, as if I was a child.

Hi? I said.

I'm not sure that it was appropriate for the gastroenterologist to stroke my hair. But by then it was quite some time since I had felt that able to draw normal boundaries between doctors and my body. I signed my self-determination away when I consented to have the procedure, or maybe on the day that I let the depressed nurse draw blood from my arm for the blood test.

The doctor put on a gown, and a face mask. He checked his phone.

I wonder if he's on Tinder, I thought.

Do you have any questions? the gastroenterologist said, when he was done with his phone.

Yes, I said. How long will this take?

This is not really a question that I had, but I felt like I should ask something, like at the end of an interview for a job that you know you don't want when the interviewer says, Any questions, and you say, Are there free snacks in the office? or Do you enjoy the commute?

Because when someone asks you if there are any questions, they'll generally feel good if you have a question, and for some reason I wanted the gastroenterologist who had just stroked my hair to feel good.

Twenty to twenty-five minutes, the gastroenterologist said, and then said, Sometimes patients with Lynch syndrome have colons that are carpeted with polyps! And then I was waking up in the recovery area.

Someone said, It's over, and someone else handed me a stack of paper. I dropped it in my lap and closed my eyes again.

The gastroenterologist arrived to tell me the results. I opened my eyes. He smiled.

You're fine, he said, I didn't find anything.

OK, I said, carefully shaping the sounds with my mouth. The anaesthetic had not yet worn off enough to return feeling to my face.

Yes, he said, you're all clear. Some people who have Lynch syndrome, their colons are already carpeted with polyps. You can come back again in two years.

You love saying 'carpeted with polyps!' I thought.

But of course I just said: Great, thank you.

So, said the gastroenterologist, how was your visit to the geneticist?

Not great, I said. He told me I have to have a hysterectomy. But I'm not going to do that right now.

Yeah, said the gastroenterologist. You know, I was thinking about you.

He paused, furrowed his brow.

And what I would do, if I were you, is I wouldn't have a hysterectomy.

In the moment this struck me as so incredible and kind, this man telling me that he wouldn't have his uterus removed. I waited until the gastroenterologist wandered off to shove a camera up someone else's asshole, and then I lay back on the bed and stared at the ceiling tiles. This time, I could not control the crying. I was silent, but the tears streaked down my face and soaked my wrap dress.

Zoe was on her way to pick me up. While I waited for her to arrive, I flicked through the stack of paper. My discharge notes. No evidence of polyps, they said. Beware of post-operative bleeding.

I flipped a page, and there in front of me was a selection of colour photos of the interior of my colon, pink and clean and uncarpeted.

I squinted at the photographs.

Maybe I'll put these on Facebook, I thought.

8

I met Martha the way that I met men in New York: on the internet. I went to a website and ticked the boxes to indicate what it was I was looking for and she came up in the search results, along with some others. Martha was a schnauzer mix, or at least that's what the website said. She was a stray dog from Puerto Rico, of unknown parentage. Found on a beach where Puerto Rican families leave the dogs they don't or can't love any more, Martha was flown to New York in a private jet by an animal-rescue charity funded by a banker who loved dogs. It was an unlikely life journey for a schnauzer mix. But Martha and I were a perfect fit. Like me, she had enormous eyebrows, and like me, she could be a little aloof, but she wanted to be loved.

When I told people that I was getting a dog, many of them told me not to. Don't get a dog, some of them said, you'll never go on vacation again. Other people said: Wait until you find a boyfriend, then get a dog. When those people said that I shrugged and said: Well, then I might be waiting for ever. I'd say it as if it was a joke, but it wasn't.

What I didn't say to people was: I've realized that I need to do what I want because I could get cancer any day now! I decided to get a dog just after my thirty-fourth birthday. I decided to get a dog because on good days I told myself that I still had my whole life ahead of me, and on bad days I thought about my grandmother who died at forty-two, and felt like I was living on borrowed time. On bad days I remembered how I used to tell people, after my dad's diagnosis with Lynch syndrome, that it was probably not nice to have an idea of how you were going to die.

Now I knew it for sure: it was not nice at all.

That's part of the reason why I decided to get a dog.

I got a dog because I love dogs and I couldn't think of a reason not to have a dog, not any more. I lived in an apartment where dogs were allowed, I worked in an office where dogs were allowed, and I made an amount of money that meant that I could afford to have a dog. I started a special savings account, for dog emergencies.

When I found Martha on the internet she was living in a foster home in Inwood, which is at the uppermost point of Manhattan, almost in the Bronx. A neighbourhood I'd never go to under normal circumstances, just because of the distance. So after I was judged by the dog adoption organization to be a suitable dog owner – You have a great energy, the woman said over the phone, and I said, . . . Sure? – I took a long subway ride to Inwood to pick Martha up and a very long and expensive cab ride back to Brooklyn, to bring her home. Martha was not called Martha when I picked her up, it seems necessary to mention, but when she climbed out of the car and we went up the stairs into the apartment I put the new nametag on her collar, which I had made in a machine at a large chain pet store the night before. The nametag was pink and heart-shaped and it said 'Martha Dogelstein'.

I sat on the couch and the dog sat on the floor and we looked at each other as if to say: Now what? We went for a walk and then another one, and then I did some work on my laptop while she took a nap in a patch of sun on the kitchen floor. At night, I put her bed on the floor next to mine and in the morning I woke up and she was staring at me again, and I looked at her and she looked at me and I thought: I've ruined my life!

But then I got up and took Martha for another walk.

I hadn't ruined my life, it turned out. I'd opened it up to something else. Now I was part of the local dog culture: walking down the street to and from the dog park, I passed people I'd seen daily for months, without acknowledgement, but now they stopped to say hello. They learned Martha's name, even though they never learned mine. Martha weighed about eight kilograms and had dark grey fur on the top of her body and light tan fur on her legs. A white mohawk grew out of the top of her head and her black-lined eyes were so big in her small head that people thought that she was a puppy even though she was two or three years old when I adopted her, the mother of two herself. I had a photo of her with her puppies, in a cage before they left Puerto Rico. The puppies went to live in New Jersey.

What's it like to be a mom? I would ask Martha, sometimes, when we were on our own. Martha would say nothing.

Sometimes people would say: What's it like to be a mom? to me, and this would make me mad. I think they were saying it because they believed that I had gotten a dog to fill the emptiness of being a single woman in my early thirties with no partner or children. I think they were saying it because they wanted to show that they supported me and my choice.

The people from whom I received the congratulations did not know, by and large, about the recommended hysterectomy.

I'm not her mom! I would say. Martha is my roommate!

Martha was a reason to rise, to move, to stare less at a screen. You're the finest dog in the land, I said to her, as we walked down the street, and I didn't care at all who heard me. If the person who heard me was also carrying a plastic bag of shit, they'd understand. If the person who heard me was not carrying a plastic bag of shit, then I didn't care what they thought. Martha's face is abnormally cute and so people stopped us quite often to remark upon it. What a cute face! they'd say; in one case, You're a little greeting from heaven! I felt proud, almost as proud as I would if they were talking about me. Sometimes, Martha would lunge at another dog on a leash, and the owner of the other dog would apologize, because Martha was so cute that it seemed like she couldn't possibly be the instigator of violence. Martha was so cute that she got away with anything.

With Martha, I told friends, I have finally come to understand what it is like to be unbelievably good-looking.

But Jean, they said, if they were nice friends, you're—

I interrupted them.

No, I said. No. I mean it. Unbelievably good-looking.

Now I didn't take the train to see my mother as often as I once did. She was busy getting ready for her move, which was just six months away. I was busier with my life in Brooklyn: I'd made new friends. I'd changed jobs. I had plans on the weekends, was taking up hobbies. But when I did go to see my mother, I took Martha with me. She had a small black travelling bag that I would put on the floor at my feet. She would sleep through the journey and then pop her head out, curious, when my mother picked us up at the train station to take us back to the Baltimore house. My mother had once been one of the people who had told me not to get a dog: she knew the reality of it, from her days as the primary caretaker to the family dog, Maisie.

Now that I have a dog, I said to my mother, I realize that when we kids said we would help with Maisie, we really weren't helping. I'm sorry!

It's OK, my mother said.

My mother was very fond of Martha, too. She gave us something to talk about. She was not the third person we wanted, but she was someone.

Was it pathetic to be a single woman who got a dog to make me less lonely? Because that is definitely what I did. Maybe it was.

One day, I took Martha to the park to meet a man I'd been on a couple of dates with, and she responded to him with intense ire: she barked and growled and wouldn't stop, which was most out of character for Martha.

It's OK, he said, when I apologized, she'll get used to me!

No, she won't, I thought.

That was the last time I saw him. Martha and I had rescued each other.

9

In Baltimore, as my mother increased her efforts to clean the house out ahead of her return to Scotland, every visit required me to go through piles of belongings with her. My old belongings. My father's old belongings. The old belongings of people that my parents had kept because they felt some obligation or loyalty to those people, not because they wanted to keep those things.

I also found a photo of Dad's grandfather, my mother said. Maybe you'd like it?

This great-grandfather was born in America, unlike my father's other grandparents, who were immigrants. He was the son of a jeweller who came from Europe during a wave of immigration that happened in the 1850s, long before things became really uncomfortable. A jeweller himself, by name and profession. A man who died, all of a sudden, when my grandfather was eighteen. Before he died he told my grandfather to study optometry and not engineering, because it was a better profession for Jews, and gave him a gold pocket watch engraved with his name.

My father died when I was eighteen, my grandfather told me once, just when I was getting ready to go to college.

My grandfather was so old at the time – at least

eighty – that it was hard to imagine him being a person who'd had a father, or lost one. Now, if I could talk to him, if he wasn't dead as well, I'd say: I'm so sorry. I get it. It's awful for your father to die.

In the photograph, my great-grandfather was wearing a nice black hat, smiling at the camera, proud, a twinkle in his eye. He had a sweet face with contours that weren't unlike mine. The photo was probably taken by a photographer on some important family occasion like a bar mitzvah, because it's not like they were a family who could often afford professional photographs. It was probably a photograph that was taken quite soon before he died. The photo was enormous. I made Martha sit next to it, for scale. The photo was much bigger than Martha.

This is a great photo, I said to my mother, but I'm not sure I can take it. If I hang it on the wall of my living room in Brooklyn, it's so enormous, the theme of my living room will become: My Dead Great-grandfather. People will come over and the people will say: Who's that guy? Why is your living room a shrine to him?

This photo will be terrible for my love life, is what I was thinking. When I said people of course I meant men, or at least a man, an unknown man who I anticipated inviting into my apartment in the hopes that he was in the process of falling in love with me.

I see what you mean, my mother said.

I mean, I said, I feel bad, because I'm sure that this was an expensive photograph for the family to have made. They probably had it made after he died. Dad's grandmother probably hung it on the wall, a special tribute.

That's true, my mother said.

But I never met my great-grandfather, I said, he died in the 1930s. Dad didn't even meet him.

That's also true, my mother said.

I remembered the time some years ago when I went to the big flea market in Brussels on a weekend trip with Frank. It was one of the weekends when Frank and I were getting along the best. At the flea market, stacks upon stacks of black and white photographs in elaborate frames were for sale: important ones. Wedding photos, christening portraits. Sepia-toned pictures of young women with Gibson Girl hairdos and young men with confident waxy moustaches.

How sad, I said to Frank, that all of these pictures are here, for sale, like trash, because the people who cared about them must be dead.

I guess so, Frank said.

I don't understand how their families can be so callous unless they're all dead, I said, I don't get why they wouldn't care.

In the basement, regarding my great-grandfather's enormous portrait, I recalled the flea market in Brussels and I thought: Now I get it. What a short time passes between people being very precious and people being unfamiliar.

Then I had a brainwave. We could send the photograph to my father's sister. At least she was one generation closer to this great-grandfather.

Let's send it to Aunt Barbara, I said to my mother, she's

one generation closer to Grandpa's dad than I am. She never met him either, but she'll appreciate it.

That's a great idea, my mother said.

Great! I said.

Great, my mother said. She smiled at me and I smiled back. Now it was a while since Dad died. Months had ticked by, and in those months, my mother and I had gotten good at solving problems together.

I went back to Brooklyn on the train with Martha. I ate another packet of eggs. A few days later, my mother called me.

I just remembered, my mother said, that a few years ago, before Dad got sick, Aunt Barbara gave that enormous photograph of your great-grandfather to us.

It was Christmas when my mother unearthed her grandmother's fur coat. That Christmas was a year and a half since my father died. A year and ten months, but who's counting? In that year and ten months, I had kind of built a life in Brooklyn, at last. I had an apartment and some furniture. I had friends and I had a dog. I went to a writing conference, travelled across the country to it. In a workshop at the conference I shared an essay I'd written about the time that my dad died and I was diagnosed with Lynch syndrome.

No offence, said a woman in the workshop, but you've kind of hit the jackpot . . . narratively.

That Christmas was quite some time since my mother

told me that she was going to move back to Scotland. I was used to the idea. My mother was slow but determined, disassembling her home with the kind of care and precision that she used to bring to removing knots from my hair. My mother refused many of my offers of help.

I'm fine, she said, again and again. I'm fine.

My mother was determined to do this herself, to shut down her life here in America, and I think I understood why. My mother was independent, like me.

The strategy that my mother had chosen to clear out the house was to hire an auction company that specializes in liquidating the possessions of people like my mother: they come round and pick through your belongings, use stickers to designate their value, and put the whole lot on the internet. Once the auction started, I visited the page several times a day, because I wanted to know what these scraps of our lives were worth to other people. Who knew that all those years I'd been sleeping next to an antique nightstand valued at $40? Who would have imagined that those scratched-up Beatles records that we'd danced to on Saturday afternoons in 1989 were originals?

My mother had already done some cleaning in the lead-up to the auction. A couple of months earlier I came down from the city to sort through my remaining possessions. Photographs that I'd taken on disposable cameras with chubby childish hands. Tatty pieces of costume jewellery. My elementary school report cards, which revealed that I was a joy to teach and very bad in gym class. Cut some time off your mile, the fourth-grade gym teacher wrote, in jaunty, legible cursive, and I thought: I had an asthma attack, bitch! and felt bad in an instant for thinking such a word about a young woman whose job it was to make children run faster. I took the report cards, though there was no reason to take them, except the thought that in twenty-five years I might look at them again and think: I had an asthma attack, bitch!

On each visit, the house was a little emptier. The recliner was still there, some of the physics mugs, but other things were gone. My father's clothes. Some of his books. His vinyl records stacked in an unruly pile, waiting for an auctioneer to pick through them, decide which are valuable and decide which ones don't matter. No one in the family owned a record player any more. I took a Benny Goodman album because the cover was pink and because no one could stop me. For now, these things were still mine as much as they belonged to anyone.

On Christmas Day my mother and I decided to mark the occasion in the manner of my father's people. It was our second Christmas without him, so we had already learned that we could survive, but that didn't mean that we were especially in the mood to celebrate. We had spent our family Christmases at home, for the most part, with Scottish traditions: presents in a pillowcase. Christmas crackers, pudding. Latkes for Christmas dinner if Chanukkah and Christmas happened to overlap.

But we weren't in the mood to do our usual things. At first we discussed going away somewhere: to the beach, perhaps. To a hotel. But we didn't. And so we behaved like Jews on Christmas. We went to the movies. We went to eat Chinese food at one of Baltimore's finest Chinese restaurants, or a restaurant that used to be fine. The staff were bustling and busy, but the room felt musty and faded. Families of middle-aged and elderly people sat around big round tables, pushing sweet and sour foods around on a Lazy Susan. Some of them had oxygen tanks. Some of them looked like they were pretty close to dying.

I had no idea, my mother said, that this was really such a thing, Chinese food for Jews on Christmas.

I bet these families have been coming since you moved to the US, I said, it was probably once a very fashionable place for Jews to spend Christmas in Baltimore.

You may be right, my mother said.

Everyone's celebrating a dead Jewish person today in one way or another, I said.

My mother and I laughed dry laughs. We ate dry spare-ribs, because Chinese restaurants were the only place where my father would consume pork. We did not complain that the shiny polyester tablecloth was faded and stained from years of use. We were not forming any attachments. This was our last Christmas in Baltimore. This was not a new tradition that we were starting: it was a kind of closure.

Back at the house, my mother brought out her grand-mother's fur coat. It was wrapped in plastic from a dry cleaner, and she carried it draped over both arms, the way that mothers carry wedding dresses in the movies. It was not a way that anyone had carried a garment towards me before: it was reverent.

Like any good left-wing woman I am a firm member of the no-fur camp. But then: in the darkest corners of my heart, I am one of those women who thinks that if you have the good fortune to inherit a garment made from slaughtered animals, maybe it's OK to wear it. In fact, perhaps you're obligated to wear it: so that the minks or stoats or raccoons – or in the case of my great-grandmother's fur coat, ponies? – did not die in vain.

Before I saw my great-grandmother's fur coat, I imagined that I would wear my great-grandmother's fur coat as I swished down the street on the coldest days in Brooklyn and people would look at me and some of them would think You murderer! but others would think: Fur is bad but let's be honest, I would wear that too if I inherited it from a long-dead Glaswegian great-grandmother. And still others would think: She looks like an exiled Lithuanian princess or former wife of Roman Abramovich.

So, said my mother, as she removed the plastic, I've tried it on already but it's not . . . right for me.

OK, I said, regarding it as it emerged.

There was something clumped about the fur. There was something wrong about the shape.

Try it on, said my mother, I'm not sure you'll like it either.

I shrugged my way into the coat. The collar was wide and made from a different kind of fur from the coat. The coat was cut as if to clothe a refrigerator. The animal skin, stiff and old, stood at a distance from my body, several inches away at some points.

I looked in the mirror.

I look like a furry refrigerator, I said to my mother.

Hm, she said, yes.

I turned this way and that.

Not like an attractive refrigerator, I said.

My grandmother was quite wide, my mother said.

I see, I said.

Yes, my mother said.

I see how it must have been very special to her! I said.

Yes! my mother said.

I bet you could donate it somewhere, I said to my mother, it's exactly the kind of thing that someone would like to wear in . . . a theatrical production.

Yes! said my mother. We could donate it to a theatre.

Or sell it on eBay! I said. There must be someone in the world who'd want this coat.

Sure, said my mother.

Well, I said.

Well, said my mother, that's fine then.

She packed the coat back into the plastic with care. There was no place for the coat in our new lives, but she was still particular.

Isn't it something, I said, as I watched her put it inside, that something so important to one person can be so unimportant a hundred years later.

It is, said my mother, it is.

Later, I tried the coat on one more time. It was still hideous. I took a selfie: I was in pyjamas, my hair un-brushed and in a knot, my mouth pursed up as if I thought I was glamorous. I thought about how the coat must have made my great-grandmother feel glamorous, how she must have worn it on occasions when she wanted to look and feel more special than she usually felt. I posted the photo on Instagram. I took the coat off. My mother put it into the auction. I checked it every day online, to see if anyone wanted the coat. At the end of the auction, someone bid on it at the last minute and got it for $6. I wondered for only a moment about who they were.

10

There was one thing that I did want from the house. My father used to call it Nanny's Magic Table. The table was magic because it folded up quite small but could also be extended to accommodate twelve people at a Rosh Hashana dinner that features both chicken and brisket, paired with Diet Sprite (for example). When my father was still alive he offered it to my sister, for her new marital home with her new husband, and when I caught wind of that from my mother I said: NO.

I did not want the table to leave the country, or maybe I did not want to not have a right to the table, just because I did not have a new husband or a new home.

I insisted that I should have the magic table. I insisted that it should not leave America, and I insisted that I should be considered a worthy owner of the magic table even if I did not own a dining room to contain it, even if I did not have a family to dine around it, even if the chances that I would be inviting twelve people over for dinner might be sorely limited by the fact that I only owned three plates. I remembered helping my dad fold the table up at the end of those Rosh Hashana dinners at his Aunt Ruth's place, pulling the leaves out and storing them in a cupboard, folding the table up so that it was the size of a credenza and replacing it in its rightful position, which was against a wall, under some paintings of Ruth's children, with silver Shabbat candlesticks on top. My mother said that I could have the table: arranged for it to be trucked from Baltimore to Brooklyn.

When the delivery men showed up in Brooklyn they rang the doorbell and looked askance at me when I opened it.

It's never going to get in, they said, it's too large! and I looked at them and I thought: What is wrong with everyone who moves furniture in New York!

I recalled the first time I moved in the city, when I hired movers from a company that was entirely staffed by artists, because I felt empathy for them, for their need for a day job. Those movers made me carry much of the stuff myself, especially after one of the artist-movers had an asthma attack when he was carrying half of my mattress upstairs. (Maybe you should do something else, I said to the artist-mover as he took his inhaler, instead of moving? and that was maybe true but also maybe not a very nice thing to say.)

Really? I said to the movers who were saying that the table was too large, Really? I don't think it's that big! All of my other furniture got through the front door! I waved my hand at all of my other furniture and the movers said, OK, we'll try, but in a tone of abject defeat. They returned to the truck. I waited.

I waited, and waited, and they were taking ages, and so I went outside to see what they were doing. They were standing in the back of the truck. I thought, Be plucky,

Jean! and I climbed up in the back of the truck with them, and it was then that I discovered that the reason the movers had been taking so long was because they were preparing to carry the largest piece of furniture that I had seen in my whole life. I don't even know how to describe it: I guess maybe it was some kind of chest of drawers, a thing that existed to store other things in the most hideous way possible. It was wooden, it was highly polished, it was rococo, and it was the size of an infant rhinoceros. Maybe an adolescent one.

For a moment I looked at it and I thought: Is this something that I forgot about? Is this a nightmare heirloom that my mother did not want to take with her to the UK? But then I remembered that I was sure: no way did this thing belong to me. No fucking way.

What are you doing? I said. That's not mine!

The delivery guys said, Really? and I said, No way! That is the size of my whole apartment! I have never seen that thing before!

The delivery guys laughed and I laughed and we all just stood for a little while in the back of the truck, laughing very hard. I doubled over.

In between laughs the delivery guys started to gasp out: Thank you! Thank you! as if they were really grateful that I was not going to make them try to shove the rhinoceros up the narrow staircase of the brownstone that contained my apartment.

They said, Thank you! and I said, No, thank YOU! and after they left and it was just me in the apartment, me with a small extendable table, I thought: I am so glad that I am not from a family where my legacy is a chest of drawers the size of a baby rhinoceros. I am so glad that I am from my family, instead.

11

My mother booked her ticket to fly out of America for the first Sunday in April. I went on the train to Baltimore one last time, to help her with the final stages. I made one last stop at the deli for one last pumpernickel bagel with cream cheese. I felt sad to be losing Baltimore. I had never lived in Baltimore, but now I didn't think I'd have a reason to go to Baltimore again.

I travelled light. The plan was for my mother to come up to New York City with me on the train. I'd help her with her luggage. She'd spend a couple of days with me in Brooklyn. Then we'd go to the airport. Arthur agreed to come too, for us to spend the weekend together, the remaining members of our family who live in America. In Glasgow, my sister and her husband and the baby would pick my mother up at the airport. They'd welcome her to her new life in an old place. As siblings we were not always aligned. But helping our mother get to her new home: this was a collective project.

If it's just me and Mum on my own, I explained to Arthur, when I asked him if he'd like to come for the weekend, I think it will be too hard and sad, but if you're there, I think we'll be able to do it.

OK, said my brother, I get it. I'll come.

He booked his flights to New York.

When I got to Baltimore, my last arrival to Baltimore, the house was nearly empty. I spent the night on a bed that was for sale in the online auction, on sheets that would be disposed of. In the morning, my mother and I drank coffee from mugs that would be left behind: the ones that did not hold important memories. Breakfast was brief, and then we left. My mother walked out of the house and locked the door and the neighbour who was driving us to the train station insisted on taking a photo. My mother smiled, and then when the photo was done my mother picked up her bag and she walked away from the house to the car, without a glance over her shoulder. I thought it was remarkable that my mother did not turn around. My mother just did not look back.

That weekend, Mum and Arthur and I did Brooklyn things: we went to brunch, we went to the park. We spent time in the neighbourhood, looked in shop windows, drank cups of coffee. I showed them around. We walked the dog. I went to yoga classes while my brother and my mother slept late.

It's great here, they said.

Thanks! I said. I was happy to be showing them at last where I lived: my home. We took a selfie on the street outside, and the three of us looked happier and more relaxed than any of us have looked for a long time. We did not talk at length about the past: we did not talk about the funeral, or how sad we'd been, or how sad we still were. We did not talk very much about Lynch syndrome. I had completed all of my appointments within the six-month cycle, and everything had again been clear.

I think Dad would be happy with my plan to go to Glasgow, my mother said, during one of these conversations, and I said: Yes.

She was right: he would be happy with this plan. Dad loved Glasgow. A thing that people say to you when someone dies is: He would have wanted you to be happy, and unlike the other clichés that people say when people die, that one is really true. Dad would want my mother to be happy. He would want us to be happy, too. That weekend, we were doing what Dad would have wanted.

The weekend felt short. On Sunday afternoon, we called a car to take us to the airport. My mother's belongings were packed into just two bags. It had been about a year since she had decided to leave America, and in that time she had divested herself of so much of what grows and collects when you are married for almost forty years, when you raise a family, when you have a certain kind of life. Now, the things that she was keeping had been shipped across the ocean, for the most part, and the rest of what she needed was here: compact.

The ride to JFK took nearly an hour. We were all quiet.

I remember, when I arrived here, my mother said, in the car, as it approached the long curving ramp up to the terminal departures entrance. Just me and little Arthur, coming to this unknown place, to this unknown life.

We smiled. We didn't say much else.

It's hard to get a direct flight from New York City to

Glasgow, as if one of the cities doesn't care about the other. My mother was flying with Icelandair to Scotland, with a stopover in Reykjavík. It's a discount airline, so the better class of seat is called EconomyComfort. Arthur and I stood back while she went to get her boarding pass, to check in her bags.

That doesn't bode well for economy, I said to Arthur, pointing at the EconomyComfort sign. He laughed, a little. It was a joke that Dad would have made, if he had been there. But if he was there, if he was still alive, we'd be somewhere else. We would not have been bidding our mother goodbye, on her own, on a one-way flight to the place where she came from.

It's not that I was trying not to cry, not exactly, but I was aware of it as a possibility, a thing that could happen. We embraced Mum and then she went to stand in the security line. We watched until she went through. In the distance, she looked small, but we could still see her waving. This time, she did look back.

Arthur's flight wasn't until the next morning. We had an evening to fill, together, even though we were exhausted. It had been years since we'd spent this much time together in just each other's company. Maybe not since high school.

What now? I said to Arthur. Shall we go to the city? To Manhattan? We can take a walk.

Sure, he said, I don't think I've been there since the time we went in the 90s.

We got a car to Manhattan, which was stupidly expensive, but it seemed justified. We were tired. Our father had died, our mother had left us in one country to go and live in another. Arthur would return to his family in California, and I would return to Martha and Brooklyn, to my job and my friends, my dates and my doctor's appointments. I would go back to being afraid of cancer. But for this moment, it was just the two of us again, Arthur and me, like it was when we were little kids, before our sister was born. After dinner, when we were maybe four and seven, or thereabouts, when our parents would snatch some time at the table to drink coffee together and talk about their days, Arthur and I would get down from the table and hide behind the sofa or in the closets in our adjoining bedrooms, whispering plots against our parents. Whatever it was that children in the single digits would plot: delaying bedtime, eavesdropping on their adult conversation. Now there were no parents to plot against; not in any proximity.

We didn't say much as the car drove us up and across through Queens and through the Midtown tunnel and into the corridors of the city streets where the high-rise buildings make you feel like you're deep at the bottom of something that is big and humming and alive.

The driver dropped us off at the edge of Times Square. We climbed out of the car onto the sidewalk. It was a Sunday night but it was still heaving with people: tourists, folks finishing their days at work, other folks starting theirs.

Wow, my brother said.

I know, I said. I held my arms up, as if I was offering

Arthur something, as if the city belonged to me. Which it did, as much as any place did. As much as I belonged to any place.

I said to my brother: This is New York!

We looked up.

ACKNOWLEDGEMENTS

Daisy Parente and the team at L&R. Francesca Main, Kish Widyaratna and the team at Picador. David Forrer at Inkwell.

Early readers, writing friends: Olivia Laing, Jessie Burton, Laura Goodman, Joanna Anderson, JoAnna Pollonais, Saskia Vogel, Helen Zaltzman, Dan Bobkoff, Ben Buckland, Emma Young, Katherine Angel, Lauren Elkin, Ellena Savage, Cathrin Wirtz, Ruth Curry, Liz Greenwood, Frances Dodds, Diana Kimball, Cassie Marketos, Jamie Coleman.

The loyal readers of 'Thread'.

Catapult and *This Recording* published some early iterations of some of what became this book.

Fiona, Arthur and Elspeth, with special thanks for their support (and tolerance).

Martha Dogelstein. Eric Winkler.

picador.com

blog
videos
interviews
extracts